Excel

ADVANCED SKILLS

ENGLISH

YEAR 4

AGES 9–10

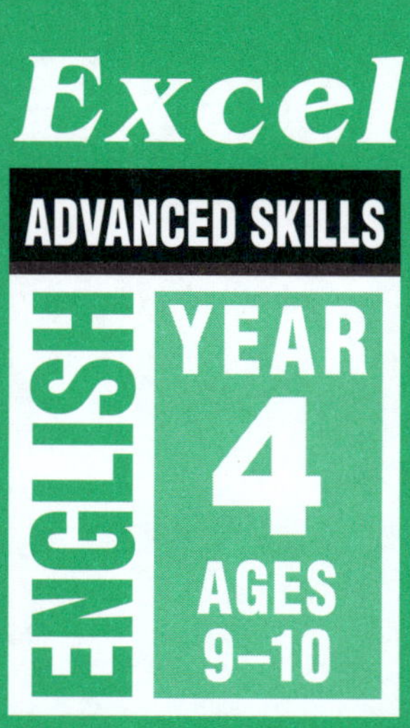

READING AND COMPREHENSION WORKBOOK

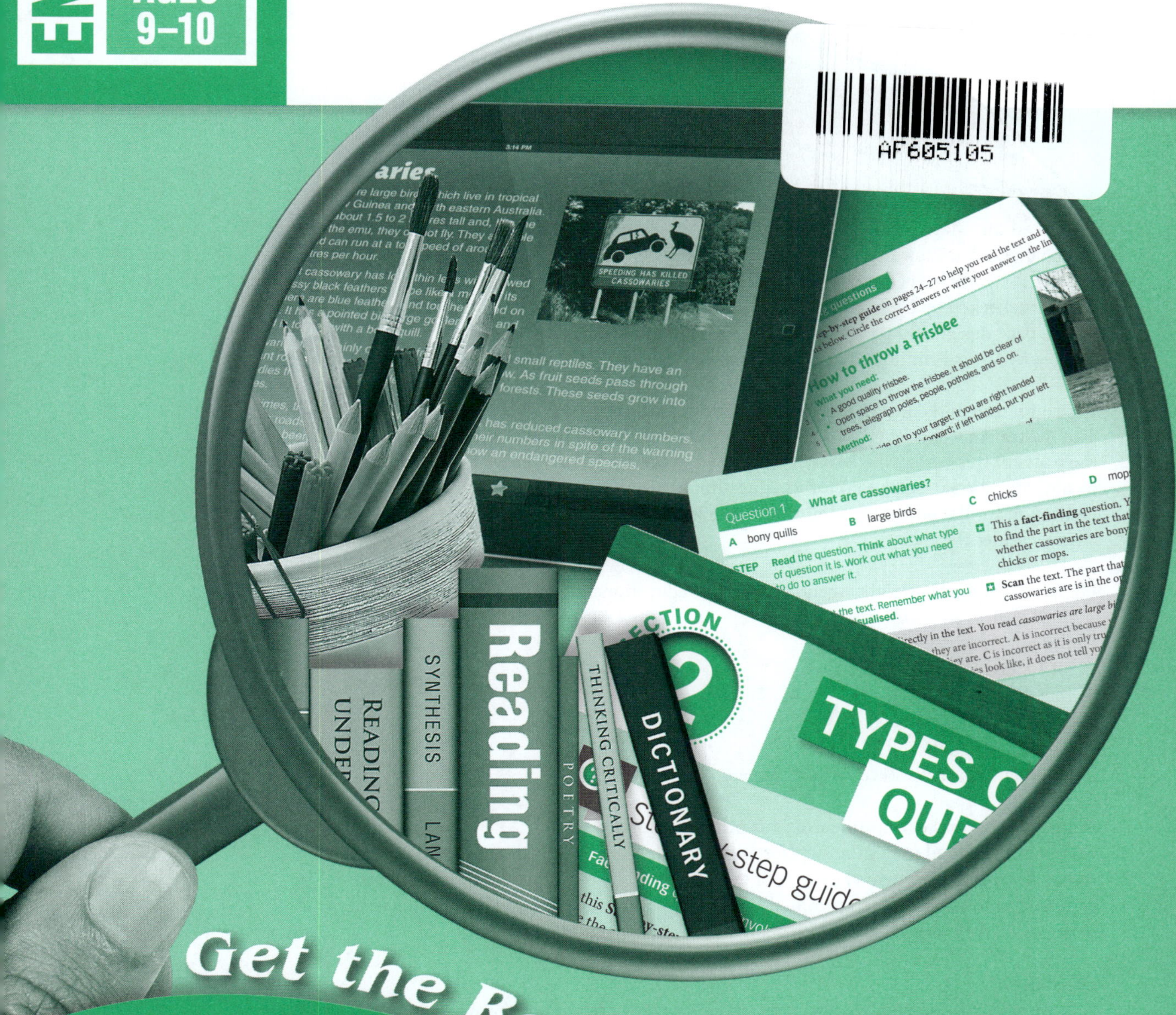

Get the Results You Want!

PASCAL PRESS

Donna Gibbs

Reprinted 2015, 2016, 2018, 2020, 2021

Updated in 2023 for the NSW Curriculum and Australian Curriculum Version 9.0 changes

Reprinted 2025

ISBN 978 1 74125 453 2

Pascal Press
PO Box 250
Glebe NSW 2037
www.pascalpress.com.au

Publisher: Vivienne Joannou
Project editor: Mark Dixon
Edited by Leanne Howard
Proofread by Michele Croucher and Mark Dixon
Answers checked by Glenda Walsh
Cover, page design and typesetting by DiZign Pty Ltd
Printed by Vivar Printing/Green Giant Press

CONTENTS

How to use this book

This book is designed to help students improve their reading comprehension skills and become more competent, reflective and critical readers.

It provides a step-by-step method of answering different types of comprehension questions, including those in standardised tests such as NAPLAN. Students are taught the strategies to read effectively.

The book is organised in four sections.

SECTION 1 Reading strategies

This section begins with a summary of the way the Step-by-step guide works for each type of comprehension question dealt with in this book. It defines the eight useful reading strategies frequently referred to. Once students have worked through Sections 1 and 2, they can use this guide to answer the mixed questions in Section 3.

Tips

- Make sure each student has ready access to the Step-by-step guide on page 4 as a useful reference when answering comprehension questions.
- Teach or revise the reading strategies of skimming and scanning, as well as ways to improve reading for understanding using the strategies of visualising, connecting, predicting, inferring, monitoring and judging (reading reflectively and critically).
- Have students complete the practice activities.

SECTION 2 Types of questions

This section deals with the five question types covered in the book. There is a chapter on each type: fact-finding, inferring, synthesis, language and judgement.

Each chapter begins with a sample reading text and step-by-step guide to reading that text and answering the particular comprehension questions.

There are five to six questions for each text. These are mostly multiple choice but at least one question per text requires a short written answer.

Tips

- Start with the chapter on fact-finding questions because these are usually the most straightforward questions to answer, depending on the complexity of the text. Judgement questions require higher-order thinking skills so they are dealt with last in the sequence here.
- Read and discuss the sample text at the beginning of the chapter. Point out the text's structure and language features. Discuss the content of the text and its purpose and audience.
- Talk to students about the type of question, how to identify it, what it's asking for and how to answer it. The Step-by-step guide makes clear to students the thought processes involved in reading with understanding.
- Discuss the strategies that competent readers use when reading a written text and answering comprehension questions.
- Discuss the answer explanations. These make it clear to students why their answers are correct or incorrect.

- Have students independently complete the comprehension tasks in each chapter.

Bringing it all together

Mixed questions

This section provides 18 reading texts with mixed question types for further practice.

Tips

- Have students complete the comprehension tasks independently in this section.
- Have students check their own answers and compare them with the answer explanations.

Answers

This section explains why answers are correct or incorrect. A suitable written answer is supplied for each short-answer question. The multiple-choice and short-answer questions enable the students to self-assess.

Tips

- Assess students' results. Analyse the patterns of correct and incorrect answers in students' results to identify areas of strength and weakness to assist with further development. Use this information to target and revise areas that need further attention.
- Identify the kinds of comprehension questions students are having difficulty with. Students from whom English is an additional language or dialect (EAL/D) often have most difficulty with inferring types of questions and questions which require background knowledge, or which use idioms that native speakers of English grow up using or knowing. English idioms can cause problems for many students, but especially students for whom English is a second language. Comprehension questions that depend on these concepts and ideas are specifically taught in the language questions section of this book.

Text overview grid

The Text overview grid on pages 123–126 provides a summary of the types of texts covered in the reading comprehension section of this book. It also offers additional teaching points and suggested ideas for student writing. Writing practice in different forms and genres will consolidate students' understanding of how texts are constructed and help them develop critical literacy.

Types of texts

The texts included in this book are defined according to their purposes: informative, imaginative and persuasive. Extracts from classic texts have been chosen to support the Australian Curriculum English Literature strand. Texts have also been chosen to support General Capabilities (Ethical Behaviour, Intercultural Understanding) and Cross-curricular Priorities (Aboriginal and Torres Strait Islander Histories and Cultures, Sustainability, Asia and Australia's engagement with Asia) of the Australian Curriculum.

READING STRATEGIES

Step-by-step guide

This section provides a summary of the way the **Step-by-step guide** works for each type of comprehension question. On page 5 you will find definitions of the eight useful reading strategies frequently referred to in this book. Once students have worked through Sections 1 and 2 they can use the guide below to help them answer the mixed questions in Section 3.

Reading the text

STEP 1	**Skim** the text to see what it is about and how it is organised.	**Read** the title. Look at the illustrations and other visual elements. Make **predictions** about the subject and purpose of the text at the paragraph, sentence, clause and word level.
STEP 2	**Read** the text. **Monitor** your reading to make sure you understand it.	**Visualise** and **connect** with the ideas in the text**. Think** about what you already know about the subject and the type of text. Make **predictions.** Make **inferences**. Reflect on meanings and make **judgements**.

Answering specific types of comprehension questions

STEP 3	**Read** the question. **Think** about what type of question it is. Work out what you need to do to answer it.	For a **fact-finding** question you need to find the part(s) of the text where the answer is stated directly. pp. 24–27 For a **synthesis** question you need to think about how ideas and information relate to each other in a text. pp. 32–35 For an **inferring** question you need to read between the lines to work out an answer that is not stated directly in the text. pp. 40–43 For a **language** question you need to work out the meaning and effects of the language used in the text. pp. 52–55 For a **judgement** question you need to make judgements about the information and ideas in the text, the writer's purpose and the values and attitudes embedded in the text. pp. 64–67
STEP 4	Think about the text. Remember what you have read and **visualised**. **Scan** the text to find the relevant parts. Look for key words or phrases. **Re-read** part or all of the text if necessary. Find answers stated directly in the text. **Infer** meanings or work out the answer using clues and evidence in the text and from your own knowledge. Think critically. Draw conclusions. Make **judgements**.	For a **fact-finding** question scan the text to find the relevant parts. Look for words or phrases used in the question. Re-read parts of the text or the whole text if necessary, to find the answer. For a **synthesis** question scan the text to find the relevant parts. Look for words or phrases used in the question. Re-read parts of the text or the whole text if necessary. Draw together the threads of meaning and draw your own conclusions. For an **inferring** question scan the text for the relevant parts. Re-read parts of the text or the whole text if necessary. Use clues in the text to help you work out what is implied to answer the question. For a **language** question scan the text for the relevant parts. Re-read parts of the text or the whole text if necessary. Examine how language is used in context. Use your knowledge of language conventions, persuasive devices and figurative language to answer the question. For a **judgement** question scan the text for the relevant parts. Re-read parts of the text or the whole text if necessary. Think critically. Make judgements based on evidence in the text and your own knowledge and understanding to answer the question.

Terms used in the Step-by-step guide

Skimming

- Skimming over the text before you start reading tells you a lot about the text and how it is organised. Skim headings and subheadings. Look at visual elements. Predict the purpose and audience for the text.

Good readers notice all of these things as they skim a text.  pp. 6–7

Visualising

- Visualising (forming mental pictures) as you read helps you maintain focus during reading, connect to the meaning of the text and remember what you are reading about.

Good readers visualise what they are reading about and store these images in their short-term memory.  pp. 8–9

Connecting

- Connecting the text with your existing knowledge helps you make sense of the text. Think: How is this story like my life? What does this remind me of? What do I already know about this subject? Have I seen this kind of text before? Where? What do I recognise about the language of the text and its structures and features?

Good readers connect to ideas in a text as they read. They relate new knowledge to existing knowledge and understanding about texts, themselves and the world.  pp. 10–11

Predicting

- Making predictions about a text before you start reading as well as while you read helps you engage with the text. Predict what the text will be about. Predict the purpose and audience for the text. If you come across a word you are unfamiliar with, use the context to predict what the word could be and its likely meaning. Predict what will come next in the text.

Good readers continually make predictions about a text and revise their predictions as they read. 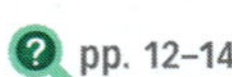 pp. 12–14

Inferring

- Making inferences as you read means working out what the writer is suggesting when it is not stated directly in the text. Writers often leave it up to the reader to read between the lines of a text. They give enough clues and contextual support for readers to be able to infer meanings. Sometimes writers leave meaning open to the reader's interpretation.

Good readers make inferences as they read, reading between the lines to work out intended meanings in the text.  pp. 15–17

Monitoring

- Monitoring your reading means thinking about the text as you read and making sure it makes sense. When you monitor your understanding of a text you realise very quickly when meaning breaks down. Re-read parts of the text to revise your understanding.

Good readers monitor their reading to maintain meaning as they read. They read on, to confirm or refute predictions and inferences, then re-read and revise understanding when inferences don't make sense. They self correct.  p. 18

Judging

- Judging means thinking critically as you read. Judge the information and ideas in the text and the ways these are expressed or implied. Making judgements about a text is an important part of being critically literate.

Good readers make judgements about a text, its context and its purpose as they read. Critically literate readers can judge whether a text is reliable, trustworthy, relevant, current, accurate, interesting, entertaining or useful based on their own purposes for reading. Critically literate readers can make judgements about the attitudes and values embedded in texts. pp. 19–20

Scanning

- Scanning means looking quickly through sections of a text for specific words, phrases or images.

Good readers can quickly find what they need in a text without having to read whole texts or sections of text. pp. 22–23

Reading with understanding

This section provides practice activities for the eight strategies referred to in the **Step-by-step guide** on page 4. These strategies support reading with understanding and answering comprehension questions.

They are:

1. Skimming
2. Visualising
3. Connecting
4. Predicting
5. Inferring
6. Monitoring
7. Judging (reading reflectively and critically)
8. Scanning.

Effective readers are able to use the strategies simultaneously without necessarily being aware that they are doing so. They make decisions about which strategies to use depending on the text and their purposes for reading.

① Skimming

What is it? **Skimming** is a useful quick 'first glance' strategy to get a general idea of what a text is about and how it is organised. Skimming a text's structure and features helps you to make predictions and judgements about the text before you read it. When you skim a text you can often tell whether it is an informative, imaginative or persuasive text. You notice features such as lists, paragraphs, columns, photographs, art work, diagrams and maps. You can skim a text to judge whether you want to read it.

How do you do it? When you skim a text your eyes move quickly across and down, or zigzag over a text, stopping briefly at the parts that get your attention such as headings, words in bold or illustrations.

For example, you might:

- skim a notice attached to a bus shelter to see if it is a timetable or a notice for a garage sale
- pick up a book titled *The Sea*, thinking it is an information book, but a quick skim through it will show you it is a story
- look for a report in the local newspaper about your school fete; you skim through the pages to find a relevant heading or a photo to locate the text you are searching for.

Have a go!

Skim the texts below. You don't need to read them. Just glance at the shape of each text and how it is organised to identify more about it. Work as quickly as you can. Choose a label from the box for each text.

poem	advertisement	newspaper article	conversation

Hobart News

21 October, 2015

Possums break into bakery

Early this morning two possums found their way into the Blossom Tree Bakery through a loose board at the back of the kitchen.

The Blossom Tree Bakery is in a small street in Hobart that backs onto a leafy lane. Mr and Mrs Flower, who own the bakery, said they are used to possums running across the iron roof of their home, which is next door to the bakery. But the possums have never before got into the bakery itself.

The sight that greeted Mr Flower, when he went to bring out last night's tray of finger buns and coffee scrolls, gave him, he said, 'a big shock'. He saw a half-empty tray and a possum that could barely move as it had eaten so much.

His wife soon discovered another tray with another possum on it. The possum was too full of baked goodies to move so much as a paw.

'No-one, including possums, can resist our cooking!' said Mr Flower with a smile.

Wildlife rescuers caught the possums. They were placed in a box and released back onto the Flowers' roof at nightfall. The Flowers have now fixed the loose board that had allowed the possums to enter the bakery.

Talking about books

Gazz: Have you read Charlie and the Chocolate Factory?

Fabiano: No. Want some grapes? What's it like?

Gazz: Thanks, Fab. Well, the main character's Charlie Bucket. He gets very excited when he wins a ticket to tour a chocolate factory because he's from this penniless family. The other four kids who win tickets are all revolting. You'd love the drawings. They're great.

Fabiano: Are they those drawings that look as if they're scribbled in a hurry but get the feeling just right?

Gazz: That's them. It's Quentin Blake. I did a project on him at school last year.

Fabiano: His drawings in James and the Giant Peach really suit the story. My dad used to read that to me when I was younger. I've read it lots of times.

Gazz: These grapes are great. Would I like it?

Fabiano: I think you would. It gets you in because after his parents are killed by a rhino, James has to live with his two cruel aunts, Sponge and Spiker.

Gazz: Whew! Does a real rhino kill him?

Fabiano: Well, real in the story. James ends up living in the peach with some weirdo friends.

Gazz: Sounds good.

A ....

B ....

Night Noodle Markets

Dreaming of some awesome family entertainment? The Night Noodle Markets could be just what you and your family are looking for.

Fragrant food. Delicious aromas to tease and tantalise as they waft by at the Night Noodle Markets.

Great locations. Outdoor dining at its best in the capital cities of Australia. Lap up the Asian hawker-style market atmosphere.

Take a peek at the menus on offer. Click on the cuisine of your choice below.

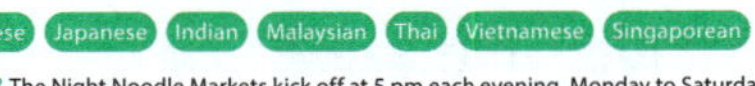

When? The Night Noodle Markets kick off at 5 pm each evening, Monday to Saturday from November 9 to 26.

Where? Download a MAP to find a Night Noodle market in your capital city.

Supported by

Drinko Soft Drinks

Nifty Noodles

Local councils

Thinking

I think that I would like to be
a possum that lives in a tree.
Or maybe much better fun,
a lizard lying in the sun.
Perhaps though I could be a bird—
I hope you don't think that absurd.
I'd like to have my own sweet nest.
Yes, I think that might be best.
Another thing I'd like to be
is something that lives in the sea.
Perhaps an octopus or whale
or a pretty fish with a stripy tail.
It would be nice to be a cat.
I'd curl up warm on the fireside mat.
Being a dog would be quite good.
Lots of walks in the neighbourhood.
In the end I s'pose it's really best
to stay myself and think the rest!

by Donna Gibbs

C ....

D ....

Answers A newspaper article B conversation C advertisement D poem

② Visualising

What is it? **Visualising** means making mental pictures or picturing information in your mind as you read. Visualising helps you engage with a text so you understand it more readily and remember what you've read.

How do you do it? You picture in your mind what is described in the text.

For example, you could:

- read a factual description of an animal and visualise what it looks like
- visualise the setting described in a narrative
- read a recipe and visualise what the final product will look, smell and taste like when it is cooked.

Have a go!

Read the lines of text taken from *When Jimbo Lost His Spots* and then stop reading. Close your eyes and visualise what you have read.

A

> 'Just look at you!' growled Jimbo's mother, a beautiful Dalmatian. 'You've been rolling in mud up to your ears.'

What do you see? What's happening? Imagine it in motion like a film strip.

Now compare what you have visualised with the answer below.

Answer You should see two dalmations standing together. The larger white-and-black spotted dog, the mother, is growling at her son, Jimbo. He is covered in thick brown mud. You might see him standing there in front of his mother, maybe with his head hanging down, his muddy coat dripping onto the ground.

B

> 'Go down to the river and wash it all off at once.'
> 'But Muuum...'
> 'At once,' barked his mother.

What do you see? What's happening? Imagine it in motion like a film strip.

Now compare what you have visualised with the answer below.

Answer You see Jimbo's mother barking crossly. You see a mud-covered Jimbo whining beside her, hoping she will let him off washing himself. As she barks her command to wash at once Jimbo turns away and heads towards the river. You see the river ahead on lower ground from where the dogs are standing.

C

> As he struggled back up the river bank, Sally, an old kookaburra, began to laugh loudly.
> 'You've washed off your spots,' she guffawed.

What do you see? What's happening? Imagine it in motion like a film strip.

Now compare what you have visualised with the answer below.

Answer You see Jimbo trying to climb back up the river bank but not finding it easy to get his footing. You see that the mud has been washed off him, but so have his spots! His white coat glistens with water. You hear laughter coming from a kookaburra perched on a branch of a tree with a view of the river bank. You see her throwing back her head and guffawing at what has happened to Jimbo. You might visualise Jimbo's dismay when he realises his spots have washed off and he suddenly realises why the kookaburra is laughing at him.

③ Connecting

What is it? **Connecting** with a text means relating it to yourself, your life and the world in which you live. It means making connections between things you already know, or know about, and the new information in a text. Connecting helps you understand and remember what you read. Readers connect to texts in different ways based on their own life experiences.

How do you do it? As you read a text you make connections with your own knowledge and experiences. You connect with a text when you think things such as:

'This reminds me of …'

'I saw something like that …'

'I've read this kind of text before …'

For example, you might:

- connect with characters in a story because you understand their feelings from experiencing something similar
- connect with outrage expressed about animal cruelty in a newspaper article because it engages your own strong feelings about animal welfare
- connect and pay close attention to information about a measles epidemic because you know that the girl next door has just caught the measles.

Have a go!

Read through the text allowing yourself to make connections with the experiences that are described. Then answer the questions that follow.

> Lunchtime. Bella swallowed down her fears. Starting at a new school was harder than she'd thought. Yesterday Janet Devine had held her nose when she'd seen her eating her salami sandwiches. She'd made everyone laugh and Bella had blushed and thrown away her lunch. Today she'd made herself cheese and lettuce sandwiches.
>
> 'Bella,' called Amara. Bella's heart stopped beating for a second then thundered on loudly. Sweat made tiny bubbles erupt above her top lip.
>
> 'Come and have lunch with us. We're going to play soccer afterwards.'
>
> A warm feeling started somewhere deep inside Bella but she didn't let it show. She knew it wasn't wise to look too keen.
>
> 'Ok, thanks,' she said moving towards Amara and her friends. She was really good at soccer. Maybe that would make them like her and they'd want her to have lunch with them again.

A Have you ever had any experiences or feelings similar to Bella's or known someone who has? Explain.

....

....

B What do you think of Janet's behaviour?

....

....

C Does Bella's story create any particular feelings or ideas in you? What are they?

....

....

Compare your answers with these suggestions:

ANSWERS

A You might recall your own first day somewhere when you didn't know anyone and felt uncomfortable. You or your friends may have been treated unkindly by others. You may recall the relief you felt when someone rescued you from a difficult situation.

B You are likely to disapprove of Janet's behaviour and see it as a kind of bullying. Or maybe you have a friend like Janet and after reading this text you realise that kind of behaviour is hurtful to others. You would hope a teacher or another girl would point out to Janet that her behaviour is unkind.

C Your own personality, background and experiences will shape your response to this question.

④ Predicting

What is it? **Predicting** means thinking ahead as you read a text and guessing what might come next based on what you understand so far. Predicting makes you an active reader. It helps you connect to a text and remember what it is about.

How do you do it? As you read you use evidence in the text to make predictions. You can change your predictions as you read on and get new evidence.

For example, you can predict:

- the contents of a book by skimming its cover
- what might happen next in a story
- the meaning of a word from its context or from reading on and finding out more
- the next word in a text using your knowledge of language patterns
- what an article in a newspaper is likely to be about from a photograph beside it.

Have a go!

1 Read the sentences below. Close your eyes and think about the predictions you make as you read.

You read: *The nurse picked up the thermometer …*

What did you predict about the nurse?

....

....

Comment: You are likely to have predicted and visualised a female nurse picking up a thermometer.

You read on: *He was taking Alex's temperature.*

How do your predictions change? What do you predict about Alex?

....

....

Comment: You adjust your prediction as you realise the sentence is about a male nurse. You are likely to think he is taking a boy's temperature.

You read on: *Alex's seventh birthday was tomorrow and she hoped she'd be well enough to blow out her candles.*

How do your predictions change?

....

....

Comment: You now know Alex is a girl so you self correct and adjust your mental picture.

2 When you are reading for meaning you do not always need to read or decode every word. You can usually work out meanings when you read on and consider word use in the context of the sentence, the paragraph or the text as a whole.

Try this.

You read: *Earthworms have the ability to replicate parts of their bodies depending on the amount of damage to the worm and where it is cut.*

You might not be familiar with the word *replicate* but you needn't stop reading and find a dictionary. You can predict that the word *replicate* means something earthworms can do when they are damaged by something. You might think about the prefix *re*, which often means 'do again'. You might also think of *duplicate*, which means 'make a copy'.

You read on: *They may be able to replace a lost tail, but maybe not a lost head.*

It becomes clear from the context that *replace* is a synonym for *replicate*.

It means that worms can sometimes remake their damaged body parts.

3 Read this extract from *Seven Little Australians* by Ethel Turner, 1912, and answer the questions about the predictions you make as you read.

> There was quite a colony of dusty boots in one corner of the room, and there was a great bottle of black, treacly-looking varnish on the mantelpiece. Bunty conceived the brilliant idea of cleaning the whole lot and standing them in a neat row to meet his father's delighted eyes. He found a handkerchief on the floor, of superfine cambric, though dirty, poured upon it a liberal allowance of varnish, and attacked the first pair …
>
> There was a step on the stair, the firm, well-known step of his father, and he paused a moment with a look of conscious virtue on his small shiny face.
>
> But it fled all at once, and a look of horror replaced it. He had stuck the bottle on a great armchair for convenience, as he was sitting on the floor, and now …

A When you first hear the name Bunty, what kind of person do you predict he or she will be?

....

....

Answer Bunty could be a girl or a boy of any age.

B What do you read that makes you confirm or change your prediction?

....

....

Answer The word *he* confirms that Bunty is male. The information that his father is coming up the stairs and that his *small shiny face* is hopeful of praise suggests Bunty is his young son.

C What do you think will happen next? What made you think this?

....

....

Answer It seems inevitable, from the moment it is described, that the *black, treacly-looking varnish* will spill. You can sense disaster is about to happen from the way tension is built. When you learn Bunty left the varnish bottle open on the arm of a chair, you guess from hearing about his *look of horror* that the varnish is about to fall off. This leads you to predict that that his father will be very cross with Bunty.

[In the book the stream of varnish falls onto his father's clothes and Bunty's father takes the strap to him. You will have noted that the text was written in 1912 when parenting customs were different.]

4 Predict which words are missing from these sentences by using your knowledge of language patterns (grammar and vocabulary).

A *The monkey* .... *three bananas and some insects for its breakfast.*

Answer Suitable verbs include 'ate', 'devoured' and 'chewed'. When you read the sentence you can predict that the missing word will be a verb and you can infer that the missing word's meaning is something to do with eating.

B *The twins cheered* .... *when their Dad said it was baked beans on toast for lunch.*

Answer You can predict that the missing word is an adverb. The answer is 'loudly' or any adverb that tells you how they cheered in support of the idea, such as 'noisily', 'excitedly', 'joyfully' or 'happily'.

C *They thought the* .... *stars looked dazzling outlined against the velvety sky.*

Answer The answer is an adjective such as bright/glowing/shining/yellow. You can predict that the word will describe the appearance of the stars in a way that shows the contrast between them and the darkness of the night sky.

⑤ Inferring

What is it? You **infer** meaning when you work out what a writer is implying or suggesting without actually stating it directly in the text.

How do you do it? You think about meanings that are implied or hinted at. You read between the lines to work out what the author is implying or suggesting.

For example, you can

- infer from the order in which events happen how they relate to each other
- infer what characters think or feel from their interactions, from what they say to each other or what a narrator implies
- infer how writers feel about a subject from their choice of language.

Have a go!

1 Read the following and answer the questions by reading between the lines to infer what is meant.

> Harold wanted to go to the Easter Show with his friends. His parents had said he couldn't go this year but he was determined to change their minds. He decided to clean their car. That would be just for starters.

A Why did Harold decide to clean his parents' car?

....

Answer You read that *Harold wanted to go to the Easter Show* and *His parents had said he couldn't go this year.* You can infer that Harold's decision to clean his parents' car is because he wants to get into their good books so they'll change their minds and let him go to the Easter Show.

B What other kinds of things was Harold planning to do for his parents?

....

Answer You read that cleaning their car would be *for starters*. You can infer Harold plans to do more things to get into his parents' good books, such as tidying his room or taking out the rubbish.

2 Read the following and then make inferences to answer the questions.

Mary had saved and saved to buy a birthday present for her mum. To get the wooden bowl her mother had admired, she needed $9.99. To get that amount she'd done lots of extra jobs and had gone without things she wanted. Mary counted her money again. And then again. Then she put it all back in her purse and set off for the shop. She couldn't wait to see her mother's face when she opened her present.

A Why did Mary count her money *again. And then again*?

....

....

Answer You can infer that Mary wanted to check she really had the right amount of money to buy the bowl. She didn't want to make a mistake and be disappointed so she counted it over and over.

B What kind of relationship is there between Mary and her mother?

....

....

Answer You can infer that Mary and her mother have a good relationship because Mary is thoughtful about what her mother would like as a present and looks forward to surprising her with it. You can infer that the look she imagines on her mother's face is a look of pleased surprise, which suggests she knows her mother appreciates her.

3 Read the text and then make inferences to answer the question.

Tom turned away from his friend. If Jake kept on putting him down the way he'd started to do lately, he'd really have to find another friend.

How does Tom feel about his friend Jake?

....

....

Answer The narrator tells you that *Tom turned away from his friend*. You can infer that he feels hurt and upset. He is also quite worried. You can infer that he is thinking of giving up his friendship with Jake unless Jake stops behaving as he's been doing lately. You can ask questions of the text: Why has Jake begun to behave in this way when he used not to do so? Is Tom to blame at all? What has gone on before the events in the text?

4 Read the text and then make inferences to answer the questions.

A message from Fred the farmer

You can buy eggs at supermarkets from hens who are kept in cramped cages or from hens free to run around in the sunshine and scratch for worms in the earth. Hens in cages have miserable lives. I prefer to eat eggs from happy, healthy hens. What about you?

Free-range eggs may cost a little more than eggs from caged birds. You have a choice. Which will you buy?

A Would Fred the farmer have caged or free-range hens on his farm?

....

Answer You can infer that Fred the farmer would have free-range hens on his farm.

B How did you come to this conclusion?

....

....

....

Answer You can infer this from the language Fred uses to describe the different methods of farming eggs. He uses emotive terms to compare the hens' lifestyles—the caged hens are *cramped* and *miserable* which shows his disapproval for this method, while the free-range hens are described as *free*, *happy* and *healthy* which indicates his approval.

C What does Fred mean when he says *You have a choice*?

....

....

....

Answer Fred says you have a choice about which eggs to buy but you can infer that he means you should realise there is only one right choice. He suggests that for a little extra money you can do the right thing and act responsibly toward animals and the farmers who farm in the right way.

⑥ Monitoring

What is it? **Monitoring** meaning means noticing as you read when a text doesn't make sense. It means thinking about the meaning of what you are reading so you immediately notice when meaning breaks down or you lose the thread of a text.

Maintaining the thread and connecting meanings across a text is part of remembering and understanding what you have read.

How do you do it? As you read you ask yourself if what you are reading makes sense. You self-correct when meaning breaks down by re-reading previous sentences, sections of the text or the whole text. You clarify things you might have misunderstood, misinterpreted or forgotten. As you read, if necessary, you adjust your predictions and rethink your inferences.

Have a go!

You read: *Hummingbirds are able to fly in any direction—backwards and sideways, up and down. They can even stop in midhair.*

If you are monitoring meaning as you read, you think about the phrase you have read *in midhair*. You decide 'that doesn't make sense'. You question the text. Why would hummingbirds stop in midhair? You try to visualise hummingbirds stopped in the middle of hair. That's not very likely. So you re-read the text.

This time you read *They can even stop in midair*.

You understand that you have misread 'midhair' for *midair*. You are not sure what *midair* means so you read on.

By beating their wings 60 to 200 times per second they can stay poised in the air without needing to land on their feet.

You work out that the meaning of *midair* is the air above ground level where there is no support for the hummingbirds' feet. This is quite different in meaning from 'midhair'.

If you hadn't monitored the meaning of what you were reading, you would have held a very confused idea about the flight of hummingbirds!

⑦ Judging

What is it? **Judging** a text means reading critically and reflecting on what you read. As you read, you make judgements about how information and ideas in a text are presented.

How do you do it? As you read, you evaluate whether the ideas and information are trustworthy, credible, biased, influenced by values and attitudes at the time something was written and so on.

For example, you can make judgements about

- an informative text's trustworthiness for particular purposes
- a website's usefulness for particular purposes
- a character's behaviour in a story
- the time and place in which a text is set
- the bias of information in a persuasive text
- an author's attitude to such matters as gender, race and culture
- how effectively language is used in a text.

Have a go!

1 Read the text and make judgements about its usefulness for the purposes listed.

> Piranhas are fish which are native to the Amazon basin in South America. Their name comes from a word meaning 'fish tooth' in indigenous languages of the Amazon. They are famous for their distinctive looking teeth. On each jaw there is a single row of blade-like pointy, triangular shaped, razor sharp teeth that interlock with each other. Piranhas are omnivorous and are famous for the speed with which they attack and eat their prey. This means that swimming in rivers where piranhas live can be dangerous for humans.

Circle the correct answer. Is the text relevant to your needs if your purpose is to:

A find out how to swim safely in the Amazon basin? Yes No Maybe

Answer The text does not have any information about swimming safely in the Amazon basin, so you would circle No.

B collect information about piranhas for a presentation? Yes No Maybe

Answer The text provides some information that could be included in a presentation on piranhas providing you can judge that the source from which the information comes is reliable, so you would circle Yes.

C collect information to advertise adventure trips to the Amazon? Yes No Maybe

Answer The text gives information that might deter travellers from visiting the Amazon about piranhas being *famous for the speed with which they attack and eat their prey.* On the other hand, advertisers may think of this as an exciting and intriguing danger that could interest tourists in adventure trips, so you would circle Maybe.

2 Make a judgement about the usefulness and trustworthiness of these websites for research into how forces act on a rocket when it launches.

Which website(s) would you consider looking at?

A http:www.buyrocketsfromus.com.au

B http://exploration.grc.nasa.gov/education/rocket/rktfor.html

C www:jo'srocketlaunchingblog.com

D http://en.wikipedia.org/wiki/Rocket_launch

....

Answer The most trustworthy of these websites for research about forces on a rocket is the government website of NASA, the National Aeronautics and Space Administration site, in the USA.

You would judge an American government website (Answer **B**) to have more accurate and unbiased information than a personal blog such as in Answer **C**.

You would judge Answer **A**, a site with an emphasis on selling rockets, as likely to be irrelevant to your research into rockets.

You would judge that the Wikipedia site about rockets, Answer **D**, might be worth looking at but as Wikipedia articles can be written anonymously by anyone, the information is not usually as trustworthy as that on more official sites, such as NASA, where experts provide the information.

3 Read the extract from *The Pied Piper of Hamelin* by Robert Browning. Use evidence in the text to make judgements about the place and time in which the text is set. Write your judgement on the answer lines.

...
Rats!
They fought the dogs and killed the cats,
And bit the babies in the cradles,
And ate the cheeses out of the vats,
And licked the soup from the cooks' own ladles,
Split open the kegs of salted sprats,
Made nests inside men's Sunday hats,
And even spoiled the women's chats,
By drowning their speaking
With shrieking and squeaking
In fifty different sharps and flats.

...
You should have heard the Hamelin people
Ringing the bells till they rocked the steeple
'Go,' cried the Mayor, 'and get long poles,
Poke out the nests and block up the holes!
Consult with carpenters and builders,
And leave in our town not even a trace
Of the rats!'—when suddenly, up the face
Of the Piper perked in the market-place,
With a, 'First, if you please, my thousand guilders!'

....

....

....

....

....

....

....

Answer You might judge that:

- the poem is set in a place called Hamelin where the currency is guilders. The currency that is used and the kind of food described (salted sprats, kegs of cheeses) make Hamelin sound more European than Asian. You might know that Hamelin is a city in Germany.
- the story of the poem is set in a time when mayors were powerful figures, countries suffered from rat plagues and men wore Sunday hats. The way the people try to deal with the rat plague is with poles rather than modern methods. This suggests that it all happened a long time ago.
- the Piper will be an important character in the poem even though we are not told much about him in this extract. He is named in the title of the poem and when he is mentioned he is described as a lively, confident figure (his face *perked* in the market place) who is ready to stand up to the Mayor. If you know the legend of the Piper who led the rats away with his music, you may recognise that this is a version of that story.

8 Scanning

What is it? **Scanning** is a strategy that helps you find specific information in a text. When you scan a text you look quickly through it to find the particular things you want to locate.

When answering reading comprehension questions it is important to read the whole text first before attempting to answer any questions. Once you have read a text, scanning can be a useful strategy for locating the information you need to answer a question. If you scan the text for answers without reading the text you might overlook important information needed to answer a question accurately.

How do you do it? Look quickly through the text to find the part you need and then examine that area more closely.

For example, you can scan:

- a text you have already read for information you need
- an alphabetical index to find your name
- a list of ingredients in a recipe to see if a particular ingredient is included
- an invitation to a party to find its date and time
- a group photo for your image
- a graph for a particular item
- a map for a place name.

Have a go!

1 Read the text through first. Then scan the text to locate and re-read the part you need to answer the questions.

Cassowaries

Cassowaries are large birds that live in tropical forests in New Guinea and north-eastern Australia. They stand about 1.5 to 2 m tall and, like the ostrich and the emu, they do not fly. They are able to swim and can run at a top speed of about 50 km per hour.

The adult cassowary has long thin legs with clawed feet. Glossy black feathers drape like a mop on its body. There are blue feathers and touches of red on its neck. It has a pointed bill, large golden eyes and its head is topped with a bony quill.

A In which kind of forests do cassowaries live? ....

B How tall are cassowaries? ....

C How quickly can cassowaries run? ....

D What colour eyes do cassowaries have? ....

Answers **A** tropical **B** 1.5 to 2 m **C** about 50 km per hour **D** golden

2 Read the text. Then scan the text to locate and re-read the part you need to answer the question.

> Dear Billy and Sabrina,
>
> Your match starts at 12.30, Billy. Yours starts at 2.00 pm, Sabrina.
>
> Both matches are to be held at:
>
> Headland Park,
> 29 Tirra Lirra St
> Greenland,
> Brisbane, 2074
>
> Here's my new phone number for if you have any questions:
> 0404 445566.
>
> The notice I read said:
>
> DRESS: Please wear your full sports uniform.
>
> btw. They want Billy to get there an hour before the match.
>
> Love
> Dad

A Who wrote the note? ....

B Who is the note written to? ....

C What time does Billy need to arrive at the ground? ....

D What time does Sabrina's match start? ....

E What phone number can the children ring? ....

F What do the children have to wear? ....

Answers **A** Dad **B** Billy and Sabrina **C** 11.30 **D** 2 pm **E** 0404 445566
F full sports uniform

Note that if you had not read the whole text first it would have been easy to answer question **C** incorrectly.

TYPES OF QUESTIONS

Step-by-step guide to **fact-finding** questions

Fact-finding questions involve finding information that is stated directly in the text.

Use this **Step-by-step guide** to help you read the text and **find facts** to answer the questions below. Circle the correct answers or write your answer on the lines.

STEP 1	**Skim** the text to see what it is about and how it is organised.	**Read** the title, *Cassowaries*. Look at the illustrations and other visual elements. Notice the illustration of the cassowary and the message it gives about cassowaries and speeding cars. Notice that the text is written in paragraphs. Make **predictions** about the subject and purpose of the text.
STEP 2	**Read** the text. **Monitor** your reading to make sure you understand it.	**Visualise** and **connect** with the ideas in the text. **Think** about what you already know about the subject and the type of text, a report. Make **predictions.** Make **inferences**. Reflect on meanings and make **judgements**.

Cassowaries

Cassowaries are large birds which live in tropical forests in New Guinea and north-eastern Australia. They stand about 1.5 to 2 m tall and, like the ostrich and the emu, they do not fly. They are able to swim and can run at a top speed of around 50 km per hour.

The adult cassowary has long thin legs with clawed feet. Glossy black feathers drape like a mop on its body. There are blue feathers and touches of red on its neck. It has a pointed bill, large golden eyes and its head is topped with a bony quill.

Cassowaries feed mainly on fallen fruit, insects and small reptiles. They have an important role in helping new rainforest trees to grow. As fruit seeds pass through their bodies they are spread widely throughout the forests. These seeds grow into new trees.

In recent times, the clearing of tropical rainforests has reduced cassowary numbers. Accidents on roads have also helped to reduce their numbers in spite of the warning signs that have been erected. Cassowaries are now an endangered species.

Question 1 What are cassowaries?

A bony quills B large birds C chicks D mops

STEP 3 **Read** the question. **Think** about what type of question it is. Work out what you need to do to answer it.

This a **fact-finding** question. You need to find the part in the text that tells you whether cassowaries are bony quills, large birds, chicks or mops.

STEP 4 **Think** about the text. Remember what you have read and **visualised**.

Scan the text. The part that tells you what cassowaries are is in the opening sentence.

B is correct. The answer is stated directly in the text. You read *cassowaries are large birds.*

Check the other options to confirm why they are incorrect. **A** is incorrect because while it gives information about cassowaries, it does not tell you what they are. **C** is incorrect as it is only true of baby cassowaries. **D** is incorrect because while it tells you what cassowaries look like, it does not tell you what they are.

Question 2 Cassowaries

A sometimes fly. B never fly. C fly occasionally. D always fly.

STEP 3 **Read** the question. **Think** about what type of question it is. Work out what you need to do to answer it.

This a **fact-finding** question. You need to find the part of the text that tells you whether cassowaries fly sometimes, never, occasionally or always.

STEP 4 **Think** about the text. Remember what you have read and **visualised**.

Scan the text. The part that gives you information about cassowaries and flight is in paragraph one.

B is correct. The answer is stated directly in the text. You read *they do not fly.* The words *do not fly* mean that cassowaries never fly.

Check the other options to confirm why they are incorrect. **A**, **C** and **D** are incorrect because cassowaries do not ever fly.

Question 3 What kind of feet does an adult cassowary have?

A clawed B long C thin D dangerous

STEP 3 **Read** the question. **Think** about what type of question it is. Work out what you need to do to answer it.

This is a **fact-finding** question. You need to find the part of the text that tells you whether a cassowary has clawed, long, thin or dangerous feet.

STEP 4 **Think** about the text. Remember what you have read and **visualised**.

Scan the text. The part that tells you what kind of feet a cassowary has is in paragraph two.

A is correct. The answer is stated directly in the text. You read that a cassowary has *clawed feet.*

Check the other options to confirm why they are incorrect. **B**, **C** and **D** are incorrect because the text does not describe an adult cassowary's feet as long, thin or dangerous.

Fact-finding questions involve finding information that is stated directly in the text.

Cassowaries

Cassowaries are large birds which live in tropical forests in New Guinea and north-eastern Australia. They stand about 1.5 to 2 m tall and, like the ostrich and the emu, they do not fly. They are able to swim and can run at a top speed of around 50 km per hour.

The adult cassowary has long thin legs with clawed feet. Glossy black feathers drape like a mop on its body. There are blue feathers and touches of red on its neck. It has a pointed bill, large golden eyes and its head is topped with a bony quill.

Cassowaries feed mainly on fallen fruit, insects and small reptiles. They have an important role in helping new rainforest trees to grow. As fruit seeds pass through their bodies they are spread widely throughout the forests. These seeds grow into new trees.

In recent times, the clearing of tropical rainforests has reduced cassowary numbers. Accidents on roads have also helped to reduce their numbers in spite of the warning signs that have been erected. Cassowaries are now an endangered species.

Question 4 **An adult cassowary's bony quill is found**

A under a mop of black feathers.
B on the top of its head.
C under its wings.
D on its pointed bill.

STEP 3 **Read** the question. **Think** about what type of question it is. Work out what you need to do to answer it.

This is a **fact-finding** question. You need to find the part of the text that tells you whether a cassowary's bony quill is found under a mop of black feathers, on the top of its head, under its wings or on its pointed bill.

STEP 4 **Think** about the text. Remember what you have read and **visualised**.

Scan the text. The part that tells you where a cassowary's bony quill is found is at the end of paragraph two.

B is correct. The answer is stated directly in the text. You read that *its head is topped by a bony quill*, which means it is found on the top of its head.

Check the other options to confirm why they are incorrect. **A**, **C** and **D** are incorrect because they name parts of the body that do not have a bony quill.

Question 5 What is spread through the forests by cassowaries?

A insects B reptiles C rain D fruit seeds

STEP 3	**Read** the question. **Think** about what type of question it is. Work out what you need to do to answer it.	This is a **fact-finding** question. You need to find the part that tells you what is spread through the forests by the cassowaries.
STEP 4	**Think** about the text. Remember what you have read and **visualised**.	**Scan** the text. The part that tells you what is spread through the forests by the cassowaries is paragraph three.

D is correct. The answer is stated directly in the text. You read *As fruit seeds pass through their bodies* [the cassowaries'] *they* [the fruit seeds] *are spread widely throughout the forests.*

Check the other options to confirm why they are incorrect. **A**, **B** and **C** are incorrect because the text does not say that anything else is spread through the forests by the cassowaries.

Question 6 What has caused cassowary numbers to be reduced?

Explain your answer on the lines below.

STEP 3	**Read** the question. **Think** about what type of question it is. Work out what you need to do to answer it.	This is a **fact-finding** question. You need to find the part of the text that gives you information about what has caused cassowary numbers to be reduced.
STEP 4	**Think** about the text. Remember what you have read and **visualised**.	**Scan** the text. Look for the part that tells you what has caused cassowary numbers to be reduced.

The answer is stated directly in the text. You read about two causes that have reduced cassowary numbers. These are the *clearing of tropical rainforests* and *accidents on the roads.* The illustration also confirms that speeding on the roads needlessly kills cassowaries.

Fact-finding questions

Use the **Step-by-step guide** on pages 24–27 to help you read the text and answer the **fact-finding** questions below. Circle the correct answers or write your answer on the lines.

How to throw a frisbee

What you need:

- A good quality frisbee.
- Open space to throw the frisbee. It should be clear of trees, telegraph poles, people, potholes, and so on.

Method:

1. Stand side on to your target. If you are right handed put your right foot forward; if left handed, put your left foot forward.
2. Hold the frisbee with your thumb on the top of the frisbee, your index finger along the edge and your three other fingers underneath in the bowl of the frisbee.
3. Aim the frisbee by extending it at shoulder height toward the direction of your target (or the person you are throwing it towards). Your index finger that is on the rim of the frisbee should point in the direction of your target.
4. Stand straight (i.e. not twisted) and relaxed. Curl your wrist towards your body. Imagine there is something on the frisbee you don't want to spill as you do this action.
5. Quickly move your arm towards your target. When your arm is nearly straight out and your index finger pointed in the direction of your target, flick your wrist to release the frisbee.

1 When learning how to throw a frisbee, you need a frisbee and

- **A** open space.
- **B** people to help you.
- **C** plenty of trees.
- **D** lots of strength.

2 You should stand

- **A** facing your target.
- **B** in front of your target.
- **C** side on to your target.
- **D** opposite your target.

3 When holding a frisbee your index finger goes

- **A** on the top.
- **B** along the edge.
- **C** in the bowl.
- **D** under the bowl.

4 Your index finger should point

- **A** beyond your target.
- **B** over your target.
- **C** towards your target.
- **D** behind your target.

5 What action is used to release the frisbee?

- **A** hold the frisbee
- **B** curl your wrist
- **C** point your finger
- **D** flick your wrist

6 What does the author say to imagine when you curl your wrist towards your body?

....

....

....

....

....

....

Answers and explanations on p. 94

Fact-finding questions

Use the **Step-by-step guide** on pages 24–27 to help you read the text and answer the **fact-finding** questions below. Circle the correct answers or write your answer on the lines.

Thinking

I think that I would like to be
a possum that lives in a tree.
Or maybe much better fun,
a lizard lying in the sun.
Perhaps though I could be a bird—
I hope you don't think that absurd.
I'd like to have my own sweet nest.
Yes, I think that might be best.
Another thing I'd like to be
is something that lives in the sea.
Perhaps an octopus or whale
or a pretty fish with a stripy tail.
It would be nice to be a cat.
I'd curl up warm on the fireside mat.
Being a dog would be quite good.
Lots of walks in the neighbourhood.
In the end I s'pose it's really best
to stay myself and *think* the rest!

1 What is the first creature the poet thinks of being?

A a tree **B** a lizard
C a possum **D** herself

2 The poet says she would like to be a bird because

A she would have her own nest.
B it would be a lot of fun.
C birds can fly.
D birds can eat lizards.

3 The poet would like to be an octopus, whale or fish because

A they can swim.
B they don't have to walk long distances.
C they can fly.
D they live in the sea.

4 The poet would like to be a cat because she likes the thought of

A prowling the neighbourhood.
B curling up in front of a warm fire.
C eating fish for dinner.
D purring.

5 What does the poet decide at the end of the poem? Explain your answer on the lines below.

....

....

....

....

....

....

Answers and explanations on pp. 94–95

Fact-finding questions

Use the **Step-by-step guide** on pages 24–27 to help you read the text and answer the **fact-finding** questions below. Circle the correct answers or write your answer on the lines.

Didgeridoos

A didgeridoo is a musical instrument. It is made from a hollow piece of bamboo or wood that is usually about 1.3 m long. The outside is decorated with traditional paintings. The First Nations people of Northern Australia have used didgeridoos for at least 20 000 years.

Didgeridoos were originally made from tree branches that had been hollowed out by termites. The makers used either a stick or hot coals to further clear out the centre of the instrument. A mouthpiece, made from beeswax or resin, was attached.

To play the instrument the musician, usually a male, squats on the ground and rests the didgeridoo on the earth. The player fills his cheeks with air and then blows this into the instrument while more air is taken in through the nose. This way of breathing and the player's vibrating lips make the pattern of sounds that is the music of the didgeridoo.

Many people think of didgeridoos as sacred instruments. This is because they are played at religious ceremonies. They are also played for pleasure and entertainment along with the acting out of stories of animals and the Dreaming. Some say that if the earth had a voice it would be the sound of the didgeridoo.

1. What is a didgeridoo?
   - **A** something hollow
   - **B** a branch of a tree
   - **C** a painting
   - **D** a musical instrument

2. What did First Australians originally use to make didgeridoos?
   - **A** hollow tree branches
   - **B** termites
   - **C** hollow bamboo
   - **D** sticks

3. What was used to further clear out the centre of the didgeridoo when it was being made?
   - **A** a stick
   - **B** beeswax or resin
   - **C** termites
   - **D** a stick or hot coals

4. The player fills his cheeks with air and then
   - **A** fills his throat with air.
   - **B** blows into the didgeridoo.
   - **C** fills his nose with air.
   - **D** breathes from the didgeridoo.

5. What makes the pattern of sounds made by the didgeridoo?
   - **A** stories of animals and the Dreaming
   - **B** vibrating the lips
   - **C** a way of breathing and vibrating the lips
   - **D** a way of breathing

6. What makes many people think of didgeridoos as sacred?

   ....

   ....

   ....

Answers and explanations on p. 95

Fact-finding questions

Use the **Step-by-step guide** on pages 24–27 to help you read the text and answer the **fact-finding** questions below. Circle the correct answers or write your answer on the lines.

HOBART NEWS

21 OCTOBER, 2015

Possums break into bakery

Early this morning two possums found their way into the Blossom Tree Bakery through a loose board at the back of the kitchen.

The Blossom Tree Bakery is in a small street in Hobart that backs onto a leafy lane. Mr and Mrs Flower, who own the bakery, said they are used to possums running across the iron roof of their home, which is next door to the bakery. But the possums have never before got into the bakery itself.

The sight that greeted Mr Flower, when he went to bring out last night's tray of finger buns and coffee scrolls, gave him, he said, 'a big shock'. He saw a half-empty tray and a possum that could barely move as it had eaten so much.

His wife soon discovered another tray with another possum on it. The possum was too full of baked goodies to move so much as a paw.

'No-one, including possums, can resist our cooking!' said Mr Flower with a smile.

Wildlife rescuers caught the possums. They were placed in a box and released back onto the Flowers' roof at nightfall. The Flowers have now fixed the loose board that had allowed the possums to enter the bakery.

1 How did the possums get into the bakery?

A through the roof
B through a loose board
C through the wall
D under the fence

2 Mr and Mrs Flower live next door to

A the bakery.
B a leafy lane.
C Hobart.
D their neighbours.

3 Who got 'a big shock' from seeing what the possum had eaten?

A Mrs Flower
B the newspaper reporter
C Mr Flower
D the *Hobart News*

4 The possum discovered by Mrs Flower was

A moving its paws.
B not moving at all.
C turning its head.
D hardly moving.

5 What happened in the end to the possums?

....

....

....

....

....

....

....

Answers and explanations on pp. 95–96

Step-by-step guide to **synthesis** questions

Synthesis questions involve connecting ideas and information from across the text.

Use this **Step-by-step guide** to help you read the text and **synthesise** information to answer the questions below. Circle the correct answers or write your answer on the lines.

STEP ①	**Skim** the text to see what it is about and how it is organised.	**Read** the title, *Save Our Planet Workshops*. Look at the illustration and other visual elements. Notice the image of the garbage bin with the arrows suggesting directions for rubbish. Notice the layout of the text includes dot points and single-line messages. Make **predictions** about its subject and purpose.
STEP ②	**Read** the text. **Monitor** your reading to make sure you understand the text.	**Visualise** and **connect** with the ideas in the text. **Think** about what you already know about the subject and the type of text, an advertisement. Make **predictions.** Make **inferences**. Reflect on meanings and make **judgements**.

Save Our Planet Workshops

Did you know that waste dumped as landfall can:

- use up our open spaces,
- release gases that pollute the water and the air, and
- harm the health and wellbeing of people and animals?

Want to stop the waste and make a difference to our planet? Get the children involved. After all, the future of our planet is in their hands. Bring your family to a Save Our Planet Workshop this school holidays. Workshops are free and lots of fun.

At our workshops we cover the 3Rs (reusing, recycling and reducing waste). Learn:

- how to make something new from something old—a sculpture, a hammock or a rocket
- how to start a swap site where you give away what you don't want and find something you do want
- how to build a cubbyhouse from used timber.

All for free.

When: This school holidays, Monday to Friday, 10 am to 12 pm.

Where: Check the Reverse Garbage website for addresses.

Let's change our future together.

The Reverse Garbage Team

Question 1 **What is the main purpose of the text?**

A to encourage people to attend Save Our Planet Workshops
B to encourage people to have fun in the holidays
C to explain the dangers of landfill
D to explain when and where workshops are held

STEP 3	**Read** the question. **Think** about what type of question it is. Work out what you need to do to answer it.	This is a **synthesis** question. You need to work out the main purpose of the text. **Think** about what the Reverse Garbage Team want to happen.
STEP 4	Remember what you have read and **visualised**. **Think** about how ideas in the text relate to each other.	**Re-read** the text. Decide what the Reverse Garbage Team is trying to make happen by publishing this advertisement.

A is correct. The purpose of the text as a whole is to encourage readers to attend Save Our Planet Workshops so they can learn more about the 3Rs.

Check the other options to confirm why they are incorrect. **B** is incorrect because while the Reverse Garbage Team want people to have fun at the workshops in the holidays, this is not the main purpose of the text. **C** is incorrect because the text is only partly about explaining the dangers of landfill. **D** is incorrect because the text is only partly about when and where the workshops are held.

Question 2 Which message is given by the text's illustration?

A Garbage collectors should take rubbish from bins.
B When your bin is full put your rubbish in another bin.
C Waste can be reused and recycled.
D Rubbish is garbage.

STEP 3	**Read** the question. **Think** about what type of question it is. Work out what you need to do to answer it.	This is a **synthesis** question. You need to work out what message is given by the illustration.
STEP 4	Remember what you have read and **visualised**. **Think** about how ideas in the text relate to each other.	Look closely at the illustration. **Think** about what each part of it means and the message that is created by how the parts relate to each other.

C is correct. The illustration is of a garbage bin with an arrow pointing out of the bin and other arrows returning towards it. This sends the idea that garbage can be reused and recycled, an idea that is important in the text.

Check the other options to confirm why they are incorrect. **A**, **B** and **D** are incorrect as they give messages that are the opposite of those given by the illustration and the text.

Question 3 Which of the following could be a motto for the Reverse Garbage Team?

A After all, the future of our planet is in their hands.
B Bring your family to a Save Our Planet Workshop this school holidays.
C All for free.
D Let's change our future together.

A *motto* is a short phrase or sentence that expresses a goal or ideal.

STEP 3	**Read** the question. **Think** about what type of question it is. Work out what you need to do to answer it.	This is a **synthesis** question. You need to select a sentence that is in the form of a motto and stands for the goal the Reverse Garbage Team wants to achieve.
STEP 4	Remember what you have read and **visualised**. **Think** about how ideas in the text relate to each other.	**Re-read** the text to decide what is the Reverse Garbage Team's goal as a group. Match the sentences in the question to this goal to select the one that could be a motto for the Reverse Garbage Team.

D is correct. The Reverse Garbage Team's goal is for everyone to work together to make a difference to the health of the planet. *Let's change our future together* is also in the form of a motto.

Check the other options to confirm why they are incorrect. **A** is incorrect. It is not the Reverse Garbage Team's main goal and it is not in the form of a motto. **B** is incorrect as it is a request to parents rather than a saying or motto. **C** is worded as a motto but its meaning is related to the cost of the workshops and the materials used for them.

Synthesis questions involve connecting ideas and information from across the text.

Save Our Planet Workshops

Did you know that waste dumped as landfall can:

- use up our open spaces,
- release gases that pollute the water and the air, and
- harm the health and wellbeing of people and animals?

Want to stop the waste and make a difference to our planet? Get the children involved. After all, the future of our planet is in their hands. Bring your family to a Save Our Planet Workshop this school holidays. Workshops are free and lots of fun.

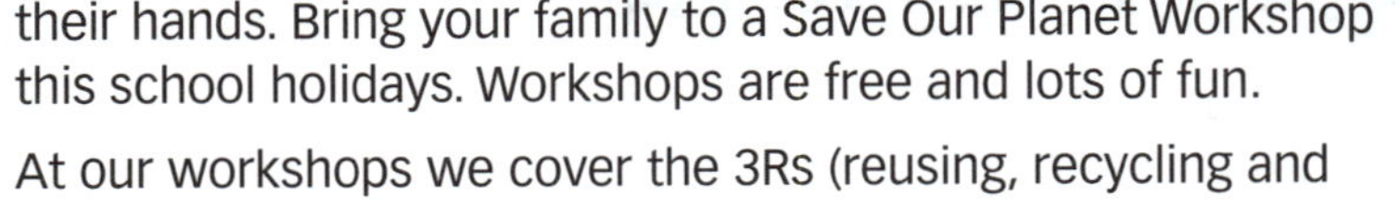

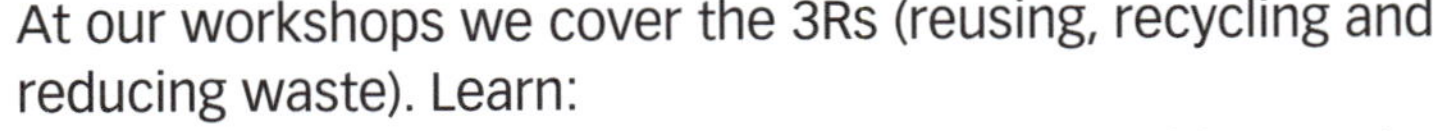

At our workshops we cover the 3Rs (reusing, recycling and reducing waste). Learn:

- how to make something new from something old—a sculpture, a hammock or a rocket
- how to start a swap site where you give away what you don't want and find something you do want
- how to build a cubbyhouse from used timber.

All for free.

When: This school holidays, Monday to Friday, 10 am to 12 pm.

Where: Check the Reverse Garbage website for addresses.

Let's change our future together.

The Reverse Garbage Team

Question 4 Which activity is NOT similar to those described for the workshop?

A Sew a patchwork quilt from old clothes.

B Make a collage from old rubbish.

C Sail a boat in a nearby creek.

D Use empty cardboard rolls to make decorations.

STEP 3 **Read** the question. **Think** about what type of question it is. Work out what you need to do to answer it.

- This is a **synthesis** question. **Think** about what kind of activities are described in the text so you can select the activity which is different from them.

STEP 4 Remember what you have read and **visualised**. **Think** about how ideas in the text relate to each other.

- **Think** about what the activities in the text have in common—they all involve reusing and recycling materials. To answer the question you need to select the activity that doesn't fit this pattern.

C is correct. Sailing a boat in a creek doesn't involve reusing and recycling materials.

Check the other options to confirm why they are incorrect. The other answers (**A**, **B** and **D**) involve recycling and reusing things so they are similar to the activities in the text.

Question 5 Which activity is similar to those described for the workshop?

A train for a marathon

B read a book

C clean your shoes

D make beads out of recycled paper

STEP 3 **Read** the question. **Think** about what type of question it is. Work out what you need to do to answer it.

This is a **synthesis** question. **Think** about what kind of activities are described for the workshop so you can select the activity which is similar to them.

STEP 4 Remember what you have read and **visualised**. **Think** about how ideas in the text relate to each other.

Think about what the activities for the workshop have in common—they all involve reusing and recycling materials. To answer the question you need to select the activity that fits this pattern.

D is correct. Making beads out of recycled paper involves reusing and recycling materials.

Check the other options to confirm why they are incorrect. The other answers (**A**, **B** and **C**) do not involve recycling and reusing things so they are different from the activities for the workshop.

Question 6 How does the Reverse Garbage Team think reusing and recycling things will help the planet?

....

....

....

STEP 3 **Read** the question. **Think** about what type of question it is. Work out what you need to do to answer it.

This is a **synthesis** question. **Think** about the connection the team makes between how learning about reusing and recycling can help the planet.

STEP 4 Remember what you have read and **visualised**. **Think** about how ideas in the text relate to each other.

Scan the text for ideas related to reusing and recycling. Re-read these parts to recall what the team says is the purpose of acting in this way and how it helps the planet.

The Reverse Garbage Team points out that reusing and recycling things avoids waste. They give evidence that dumped waste is harmful to the planet. They show that saving the earth's resources helps the planet by adding less waste to landfill.

Synthesis questions

Use the **Step-by-step guide** on pages 32–35 to help you read the text and answer the **synthesis** questions below. Circle the correct answers or write your answer on the lines.

Our excursion to Chinatown

On a windy day in June, Fourth Class caught the train to Chinatown. We had begun to learn Mandarin and our teacher said this excursion would let us practise our language skills and learn more about Chinese culture.

We entered Chinatown through the arched entrance gate with red painted wooden pillars. Big stone beasts sat on each side. I noticed that the street signs were written in both Chinese and English. I photographed the sign for Hay Street.

The next place we visited was the Chinese Garden of Friendship which was very peaceful. There were waterfalls, hidden stone pathways and a beautiful teahouse.

At last it was time for our Chinese lunch. We entered an enormous restaurant that had red lanterns hanging from the roof and red dragons on the walls. The waiters greeted us in Mandarin and we answered them in Mandarin. We were shown how to use chopsticks and how to choose from the menus with Chinese writing.

At 2.30 we said zài jiàn (goodbye) to Chinatown. We were all very tired. One person, who I won't name, fell asleep on the train and snored loudly. He blushed red when he woke up!

Tom Gagen, Fourth Class

1. What is the main purpose of this text?
   - **A** to describe Chinese culture
   - **B** to describe Tom's favourite Chinese meals
   - **C** to retell what happened on the excursion to Chinatown
   - **D** to give information about Chinese eating customs

2. What was the first thing linked to Chinese culture that the students saw on their excursion?
   - **A** the teahouse
   - **B** the arched entrance gate with stone beasts on either side
   - **C** the street signs
   - **D** chopsticks.

3. Which activity did NOT help students practise their language skills?
   - **A** reading the street signs
   - **B** talking with the waiters at lunch
   - **C** visiting the Chinese Garden of Friendship
   - **D** saying goodbye to Chinatown

4. The colour red is mentioned four times in the text. Which example is different from the others?
   - **A** the red painted pillars of the entrance gate
   - **B** the student's red face
   - **C** the red lanterns in the restaurant
   - **D** the red dragons in the restaurant

5. Tom's recount is too long to be published in the school newsletter. Which two sentences should he edit out? Explain your choice.

....

....

....

....

....

....

....

Answers and explanations on p. 96

Synthesis questions

Use the **Step-by-step guide** on pages 32–35 to help you read the text and answer the **synthesis** questions below. Circle the correct answers or write your answer on the lines.

The First Hurdle

Feeling brave and confident, with the magic spell in her head, Willa set off to find a path through the forest to the Rainbow Dragon's lair. When she'd travelled a short distance, she heard something thrashing its way towards her through the undergrowth. It gave a high-pitched wail. Large goose bumps broke out on Willa's arms and legs. She ignored them, plucked a stalk of grass and chewed on it lazily.

A tall green, red and purple creature skidded to a halt in front of her. Willa nearly swallowed the stalk of grass whole. This thing was mega-tall and mega-ferocious and had saliva dripping from its tentacles.

'I am a Killer Plant from the forest. I swallow 20 men in one gulp for breakfast and 50 in two gulps for my supper.'

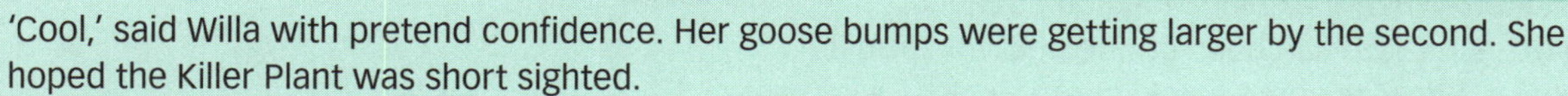

'Cool,' said Willa with pretend confidence. Her goose bumps were getting larger by the second. She hoped the Killer Plant was short sighted.

'I just saw 50 men playing cards down by the lake. They'd make a delicious supper for you,' she said, turning away. 'Have a good day,' she added.

'Whew!' Willa whispered to herself when she heard the Killer Plant thrashing towards the lake. 'First hurdle over, I h-h-h-hope.'

From *The Rainbow Dragon* by Donna Gibbs

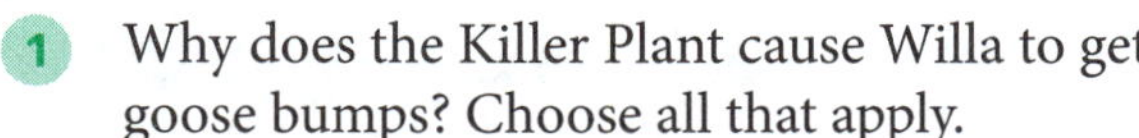

1 Why does the Killer Plant cause Willa to get goose bumps? Choose all that apply.

- **A** It is boastful and foolish.
- **B** It has a high-pitched wail.
- **C** It moves slowly.
- **D** It says it eats humans every day.

2 Willa speaks confidently to the Killer Plant because

- **A** she doesn't want it to know she is afraid.
- **B** she's feeling clever.
- **C** she is sure she can escape from it.
- **D** it likes confident people.

3 Which of the following occurs last in time?

- **A** Willa notices saliva dripping from the Killer Plant's tentacles.
- **B** The Killer Plant thrashes towards the lake.
- **C** Willa hears something thrashing towards her.
- **D** Willa's goose bumps increase in size.

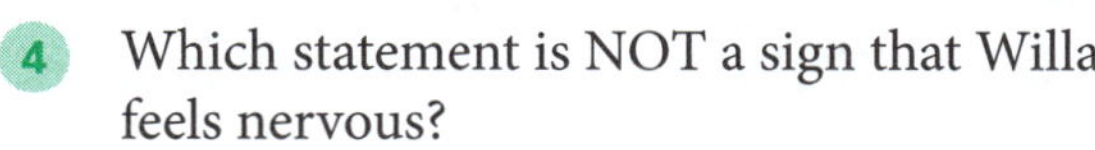

4 Which statement is NOT a sign that Willa feels nervous?

- **A** She is pleased to have the magic spell in her head.
- **B** She gets goosebumps.
- **C** She chews lazily on the grass stalk.
- **D** She stutters when she says the word *h-h-h-hope.*

5 Willa is the heroine of the story because

- **A** the Rainbow Dragon honours her actions.
- **B** she uses the magic spell.
- **C** she outwits the Killer Plant with courage and cunning.
- **D** she is a girl.

6 What role does the Killer Plant have in the story?

....

....

....

Answers and explanations on pp. 96–97

Synthesis questions

Use the **Step-by-step guide** on pages 32–35 to help you read the text and answer the **synthesis** questions below. Circle the correct answers or write your answer on the lines.

Elizabeth Haywood: a survivor

Elizabeth Haywood was born in 1773 in Stepney, Great Britain. She became a clogmaker and in 1786, when she was 13, she stole a linen gown, a silk bonnet and a bath cloak from her employer. These were pawned by her to get money for food. She was found guilty of theft and sentenced to transportation to Australia for seven years.

Elizabeth was the youngest female convict on the first fleet. She sailed on the *Lady Penrhyn*, one of 11 ships to make the journey to Sydney Cove. The 101 female convicts on board were kept in overcrowded conditions and were poorly treated. When the ship landed on 26 January 1788, Elizabeth had been on the boat for almost a year. She was immediately put to work as a servant.

Two years later, she was punished with 30 lashes 'for insolence' to her employer and sent to Norfolk Island. She survived a shipwreck along the way. In 1813, Governor Macquarie rewarded a well-behaved group from Norfolk Island, which included Elizabeth, by settling them in Van Diemen's Land* with their own land grant and a two-year supply of food, clothing and convict labourers.

With her partner David Gibson, she had ten children. They lived together in Pleasant Banks in the historic town of Evandale. She died in 1836.

* Van Diemen's Land is now called Tasmania.

1. The main purpose of the text is to give an account of
   - **A** the first fleet.
   - **B** convict life.
   - **C** Elizabeth Haywood's life.
   - **D** Norfolk Island.

2. Paragraph one is mainly about
   - **A** Elizabeth's family.
   - **B** Elizabeth's favourite activities.
   - **C** Elizabeth's good behaviour.
   - **D** events from Elizabeth's early life.

3. Which statement is NOT true?
   - **A** Elizabeth had the choice of travel.
   - **B** Elizabeth was made a servant.
   - **C** Elizabeth was lashed for bad behaviour.
   - **D** Elizabeth was poorly treated on the first fleet.

4. How long did Elizabeth spend on Norfolk Island?
   - **A** 23 years
   - **B** 33 years
   - **C** ten years
   - **D** a lifetime

5. Why does the title describe Elizabeth Hayward as *a survivor*?

   ....

   ....

   ....

   ....

   ....

   ....

Answers and explanations on p. 97

Synthesis questions

Use the **Step-by-step guide** on pages 32–35 to help you read the text and answer the **synthesis** questions below. Circle the correct answers or write your answer on the lines.

Sculpture by the Sea

Each year in early summer the coastal track between Bondi Beach and Tamarama in Sydney is dotted with a series of eye-catching sculptures. They don't just grow there, of course. They are part of the *Sculpture by the Sea* exhibition.

This free event was dreamed up by David Handley. The idea was sparked by his visit to an outdoor sculpture park set in 13th-century ruins in Bohemia. Eventually with the support of many people, Handley's dream became a reality.

Sculpture by the Sea has been an annual event since 1997. It offers sculptors a chance to have their work seen by a huge audience—up to half a million people walk the coastal track to see the exhibition each year. This means sculptors can have their work seen by more people than they could expect from a lifetime of gallery exhibitions.

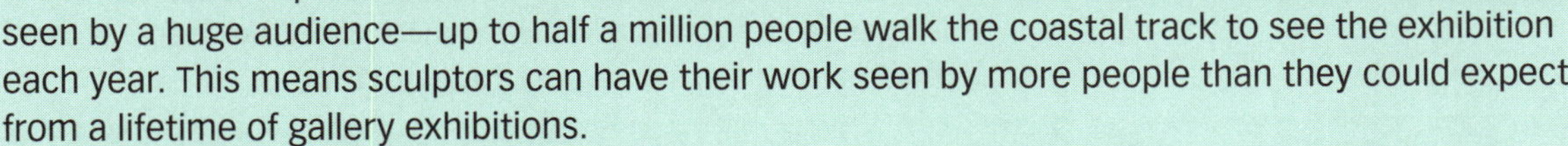

The success of the Sydney event has led to its uptake in other Australian states and in 2009, Crown Prince Frederick and his Australian wife, Crown Princess Mary, after seeing the Sydney exhibition, launched a similar free annual event held along the scenic Aarhus coastline in Denmark.

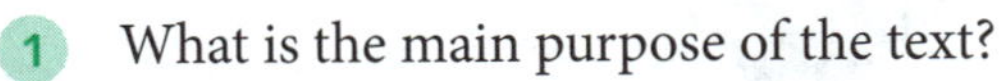

1. What is the main purpose of the text?
   - **A** to describe how to create a sculpture
   - **B** to give information about an event
   - **C** to give directions to Bondi Beach to see Sculpture by the Sea
   - **D** to encourage sculptors to show their work

2. Which of the following occurred first in time?
   - **A** the first Sculpture by the Sea held in Australia
   - **B** Handley's visit to Bohemia
   - **C** the first Sculpture by the Sea held in Denmark
   - **D** the 2014 Sculpture by the Sea event

3. Which information is NOT included in the text?
   - **A** the name of the man who dreamed up the event
   - **B** the number of people who attend the event
   - **C** the cost of attending the event
   - **D** how sculptors can enter their work in the event

4. What could be added to make the information useful to tourists wanting to visit the exhibition?
   - **A** details about the prizes on offer
   - **B** details about Princess Mary's visit to Sculpture by the Sea
   - **C** details about its dates and how to find the venue
   - **D** details about the 13th-century ruins in Bohemia

5. What do the Sydney and Aarhus Sculpture by the Sea events have in common?

Answers and explanations on pp. 97–98

Step-by-step guide to **inferring** questions

Inferring questions involve reading between the lines to work out an answer that is not stated directly in the text.

Use this **Step-by-step guide** to help you read the text and make **inferences** to answer the questions below. Circle the correct answers or write your answers on the lines.

STEP 1	**Skim** the text to see what it is about and how it is organised.	**Read** the title, *Is there a Loch Ness monster?* Look at the illustrations and other visual elements. Notice the cartoon-like picture of the Loch Ness monster and **predict** what it suggests about the text. Make **predictions** about the subject and purpose of the text.
STEP 2	**Read** the text. **Monitor** your reading to make sure you understand the text.	**Visualise** and **connect** with the ideas in the text. **Think** about what you already know about the subject and the type of text, a discussion. Notice that the title is a question. Notice that it is written in paragraphs. Make **predictions.** Make **inferences**. Reflect on meanings and make **judgements**.

Is there a Loch Ness Monster?

About 1500 years ago the Picts carved a strange-looking creature into a crop of stone near Loch Ness in Scotland. Since then people have wondered whether a monster lives in its depths.

Some people are sure that 'Nessie' lives there. Many people say they have seen a dinosaur-like creature raising its head and parts of its enormous body above the surface of the lake.

The lake is fed by seven major rivers. The population of the world could fit into it many times over. This is why some think no-one can find Nessie.

Other people think that Nessie is nothing more than a myth. They argue there is no way a dinosaur could have survived because the lake was frozen over during the ice ages. They think people are tricked into believing they see a monster when it is just a hoax or a disturbance in the water. Their strongest argument is that there is still no real evidence. They point out that although scientists have attempted to settle the question by using sonar equipment to search the deep, they have failed to find the monster. However, they did find moving underwater objects they couldn't explain.

Maybe one day, further down the track, we will know for sure whether Nessie really does exist.

Question 1 **Why did the stone carving make people wonder if a monster lives in the lake?**

A There are carvings of strange creatures all over Scotland.
B The carving could have been a picture of something seen in the lake.
C The stone is near the lake.
D The stone carving is very old.

STEP		
STEP 3	**Read** the question. **Think** about what type of question it is. Work out what you need to do to answer it.	This is an **inferring** question. The answer is not stated directly in the text. You need to work out why a carving of a strange creature would make people wonder if a monster lives in the lake.
STEP 4	**Think** about the text. Remember what you have read and **visualised**.	**Scan** the text to find the part about the stone carving being found. Re-read that part of the text to **infer** what it is about the carving that would cause people to wonder if a monster lives in the lake.

B is correct. You can infer that people thought the carving of a *strange-looking creature* was a picture of something that had been seen alive and living in the lake.

Check the other options to confirm why they are incorrect. **A** is incorrect because the text is about a particular carving on stone near Loch Ness—other stone carvings are not mentioned. **C** is part of the reason but without the picture of a strange creature being on the stone, people would not have wondered if a monster lived in the lake. **D** is incorrect because the age of the stone doesn't explain the link between the carving on the stone and the idea that a monster lives in the lake.

Question 2 Why do some people think Nessie can't be found in the lake?

A Nessie is good at disguise.
B Nessie has left the lake and lives in a major river.
C Nessie chooses to stay hidden.
D The lake is so huge that Nessie can't be found.

STEP		
STEP 3	**Read** the question. **Think** about what type of question it is. Work out what you need to do to answer it.	This is an **inferring** question. The answer is not stated directly in the text. You need to read between the lines and work out why some people think Nessie can't be found in the lake.
STEP 4	Remember what you have read and **visualised**.	Re-read what is said about the lake to **infer** why Nessie can't be found there.

D is correct. You read that the lake *is fed by seven major rivers* and *The population of the world could fit into it many times over*. This means the lake is enormous. It is implied that the huge size of the lake is a reason for some people thinking that Nessie hasn't yet been found.

Check the other options to confirm why they are incorrect. **A** is incorrect because no-one suggests the reason Nessie can't be found is because it is good at disguise. **B** is incorrect because no-one suggests Nessie is living in a major river. **C** is incorrect because nobody knows what Nessie chooses to do.

Question 3 Which is NOT a reason for thinking Nessie is a myth?

A A dinosaur couldn't have survived in a lake during the ice ages.
B People have been tricked into thinking there is a sea monster in the lake.
C Nessie looks like a creature from out of space.
D There is no real evidence that Nessie exists.

STEP		
STEP 3	**Read** the question. **Think** about what type of question it is. Work out what you need to do to answer it.	This is an **inferring** question. The answer is not stated directly in the text. You need to work out which is NOT a reason for thinking Nessie is a myth.
STEP 4	Remember what you have read and **visualised**.	Re-read the reasons given for thinking Nessie is a myth. **Think** about which statement is different from these.

C is correct. No-one knows for sure how Nessie looks. Nessie's appearance is not a reason for thinking she is a myth.

Check the other options to confirm why they are incorrect. **A**, **B** and **D** are incorrect. They are all reasons given for thinking Nessie is a myth.

Step-by-step guide to **inferring** questions *continued*

Inferring questions involve reading between the lines to work out an answer that is not stated directly in the text.

Is there a Loch Ness Monster?

About 1500 years ago the Picts carved a strange-looking creature into a crop of stone near Loch Ness in Scotland. Since then people have wondered whether a monster lives in its depths.

Some people are sure that 'Nessie' lives there. Many people say they have seen a dinosaur-like creature raising its head and parts of its enormous body above the surface of the lake.

The lake is fed by seven major rivers. The population of the world could fit into it many times over. This is why some think no-one can find Nessie.

Other people think that Nessie is nothing more than a myth. They argue there is no way a dinosaur could have survived because the lake was frozen over during the ice ages. They think people are tricked into believing they see a monster when it is just a hoax or a disturbance in the water. Their strongest argument is that there is still no real evidence. They point out that although scientists have attempted to settle the question by using sonar equipment to search the deep, they have failed to find the monster. However, they did find moving underwater objects they couldn't explain.

Maybe one day, further down the track, we will know for sure whether Nessie really does exist.

Question 4 **It is thought people make up hoaxes about Nessie because**

A they want to have fun.
B they want to trick people into believing a monster is in the lake.
C they want to test whether there is a monster in the lake.
D they enjoy being unkind.

STEP 3 **Read** the question. **Think** about what type of question it is. Work out what you need to do to answer it.

- This is an **inferring** question. The answer is not stated directly in the text. You need to read between the lines to work out why people make up hoaxes.

STEP 4 Remember what you have read and **visualised**.

- Re-read the part about people making up hoaxes to **infer** why they do this.

B is correct. You read *They think people are tricked into believing they see a monster when it is just a hoax.* This suggests that people hoax others in order to trick them into believing there is a monster in the lake.

Check the other options to confirm why they are incorrect. **A** is partly correct because a hoax is usually done for fun, but the main reason given is that the hoax is done to trick others. **C** is incorrect because the hoax aims to trick people, not to test or prove anything. **D**, that people enjoy being unkind, may or may not be true, but this is not suggested as a reason for the hoaxes.

Question 5 Scientists have failed to find the monster because

A their sonar equipment broke down.
B the monster kept itself hidden from them.
C their sonar equipment needed replacing.
D the evidence they found is not proof either way.

STEP 3 **Read** the question. **Think** about what type of question it is. Work out what you need to do to answer it.

- This is an **inferring** question. The answer is not stated directly in the text. You need to read between the lines to work out why scientists have failed to prove that there is a monster in the lake.

STEP 4 Remember what you have read and **visualised**.

- **Scan** the text to find the paragraph about the evidence found by the scientists. Re-read the paragraph to work out what is implied about what the scientists found out. **Think** about what this suggests about why the scientists failed to prove that there is a monster in the lake.

D is correct. The evidence scientists found does not yet *settle the question*. This is because while they found no evidence of a monster, there were underwater objects they couldn't identify which may have been a monster.

Check the other options to confirm why they are incorrect. **A** and **C** are incorrect as there is no evidence in the text that the sonar equipment broke down or needed replacing. **B** assumes there is a monster so this can't be used as evidence for why scientists failed to find it.

Question 6 Why does the author think *Maybe one day … we will know for sure whether Nessie really does exist*?

Explain your answer on the lines below.

....

....

....

STEP 3 **Read** the question. **Think** about what type of question it is. Work out what you need to do to answer it.

- This is an **inferring** question. The answer is not stated directly in the text. You need to read between the lines to work out why the author thinks *Maybe one day … we will know for sure*.

STEP 4 Remember what you have read and **visualised**.

- **Scan** the text to find the sentence beginning with *Maybe one day*. Re-read it to **infer** how the future might change to make the author think this.

Your answer needs to explain that the only thing that can really change in the future (*one day*) is the scientific equipment and methods used for testing. The author is thinking that improvements of this kind might lead people to find out *for sure* whether or not there is a monster in the lake.

Inferring questions

Use the **Step-by-step guide** on pages 40–43 to help you read the text and answer the **inferring** questions below. Circle the correct answers or write your answer on the lines.

My trip to South America

From: Theo@globalbackpackers.com
Subject: My trip to South America
To: Susie Bloomfield<susiel@hereandnow.com.au>

Dear Mum, Dad and Little Sis

Since I left Oz I have visited several countries in South America and seen some amazing sights. Last week I swam in the Atlantic at Ipanema Beach in Rio de Janeiro, Brazil. Do you remember 'The Girl from Ipanema'—I sang that while I swam!

I also went hiking with some friends along the Inca Trail through the Andes in Peru. When we were on the highest pass we were 4200 m above sea level. The scenery was amazing. The highlight came when we reached Machu Picchu, the lost city of the Incas. It was built around 1450 but abandoned during the Spanish Conquest of the Inca Empire. Over the centuries, jungle grew over the site. Now, since being rediscovered, Machu Picchu is a big tourist attraction. That's a worry though because it's hard to protect the environment with so many visitors tramping around.

There is still one place I'd like to visit—Easter Island with all those enormous statues. Some are as high as 4 m and weigh 14 000 kg, I'm told. If I find time to visit Chile, I might get to Easter Island from Santiago de Chile.

I'll say *adios* for now. See how my Spanish is improving!

Love
Theo

1 The two countries Theo has visited in South America are

A Ipanema and Rio de Janeiro.
B Rio Janeiro and Brazil.
C Brazil and Peru.
D Peru and Chile.

2 The Girl from Ipanema is

A a girl Theo met in Brazil.
B a girl Theo met in Australia.
C a song about a girl.
D a Brazilian statue.

3 The Andes referred to in paragraph two are

A a race of people. **B** mountains.
C walking tracks. **D** a group of lakes.

4 The Incas are

A people from a very old civilisation.
B people from a very new civilisation.
C Theo's friends who went on the hike.
D people Theo knows.

5 The text mentions *the Spanish Conquest of the Inca Empire*. What evidence is there that the conquest, from a Spanish point of view, was successful?

....

....

....

....

Answers and explanations on p. 98

Inferring questions

Use the **Step-by-step guide** on pages 40–43 to help you read the text and answer the **inferring** questions below. Circle the correct answers or write your answer on the lines.

Life cycle of the frog

The female frog lays 20 000 or more eggs in the water and covers them with a jelly-like substance. This mass of eggs, or frogspawn, is left floating in the water. Only a few of these eggs survive.

The yolk in each egg splits into two cells and then divides into four, eight, and so on, to form an embryo. The embryo feeds on its jelly-like covering. A few weeks later, it hatches into a small tadpole with underdeveloped gills, a tiny mouth and a long tail.

Each stage of development from egg to frog has dangers. It may be eaten by other water animals. In places where rains are seasonal, it may not have enough water to survive.

After about four weeks, the tadpole's gills begin to be grown over by skin. Then after five weeks it starts to grow hind legs and bulges appear where its front legs are growing. Its tail becomes smaller and its lungs begin to develop.

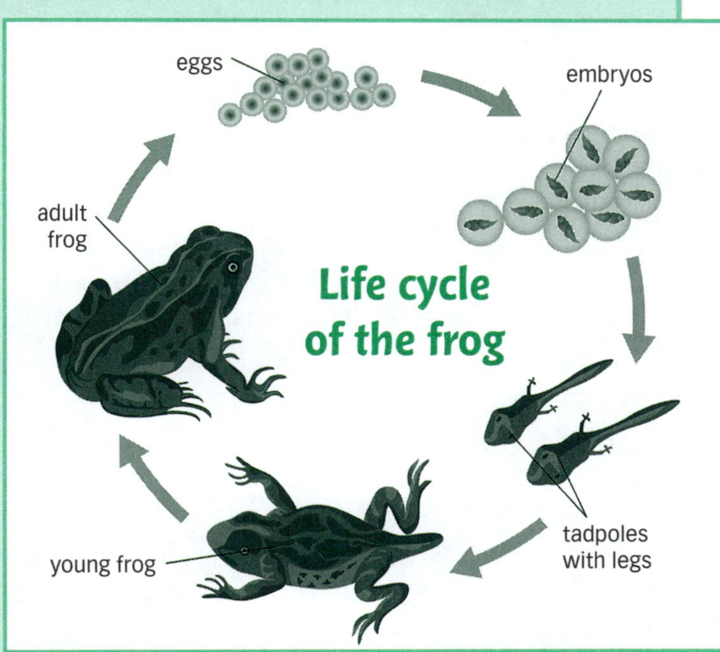

By around 11 weeks a froglet has only a stub of tail left. A few weeks later, when it is fully grown, it will live mostly on land. In the spring male frogs croak loudly to attract females. They mate and the process begins all over again.

1 Why do only a few frog eggs survive? Choose all that apply.

A They are eaten by other water animals.
B They drown in the water.
C The adult frogs don't stay with the eggs to protect them.
D They turn into jelly.

2 What number of cells will there be when the eight cells divide again?

A 24 **B** 32
C 16 **D** 12

3 Tadpoles grow legs mainly because

A they need legs for hopping on land when they become frogs.
B they help them swim quickly.
C they help them escape predators in the water.
D they use them as flippers for speed.

4 Why does a frog have lungs?

A They are needed for swimming.
B They are needed to breathe on land.
C It uses them to catch insects.
D They let them stay underwater for a long time.

5 What are the main differences between the body of a tadpole and that of a frog?

....

....

....

....

....

Answers and explanations on pp. 98–99

Inferring questions

Use the **Step-by-step guide** on pages 40–43 to help you read the text and answer the **inferring** questions below. Circle the correct answers or write your answer on the lines.

The Second Hurdle

As Willa stepped out from the shade of the forest into the dazzling light, she almost stumbled into a deep, dark chasm. Steadying herself, she peered into its eerie depths. It was deeper than a bottomless pit and wider than the sun.

This was only the second hurdle of her journey, yet it looked as if it might defeat her. No-one could cross a chasm so vast!

A loud flapping noise made Willa look up. A giant bird hovered above her. It was a pterosaur she was certain! She'd read about one in the newspaper quite recently.

'Want to get to the other side of that pit?' croaked the bird.

'Yes, please,' Willa replied politely. What else could she say to a pterosaur who'd arrived unexpectedly out of the age of the dinosaurs?

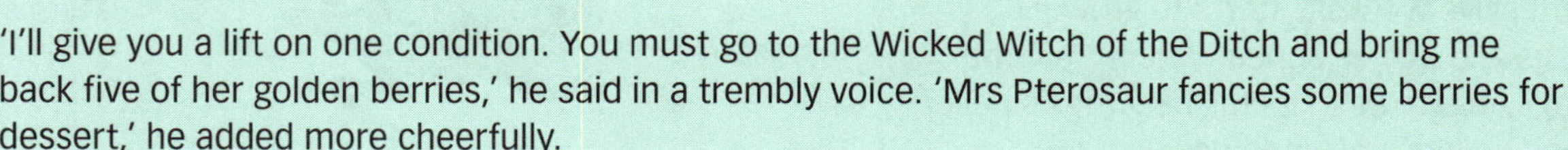

'I'll give you a lift on one condition. You must go to the Wicked Witch of the Ditch and bring me back five of her golden berries,' he said in a trembly voice. 'Mrs Pterosaur fancies some berries for dessert,' he added more cheerfully.

'No problems. Let's go.' Willa replied. Witches were only in story books, weren't they? Willa swallowed down her doubts. Anyway, it was too late to turn back now.

From *The Rainbow Dragon* by Donna Gibbs

1 Why did Willa nearly fall into the chasm?

- **A** It was a bottomless pit.
- **B** The chasm had eerie depths.
- **C** The light dazzled her so she didn't see it at first.
- **D** She was unsteady on her feet.

2 Why is the pterosaur able to cross the chasm when Willa can't?

- **A** The pterosaur is very powerful.
- **B** The pterosaur can fly.
- **C** The pterosaur has magic powers.
- **D** The pterosaur knows of a secret path.

3 How did Willa know that the pterosaur came from the age of the dinosaurs?

- **A** It looked old.
- **B** She had never seen a live pterosaur.
- **C** It had a croaky voice.
- **D** She had learned about pterosaurs from a newspaper she'd read.

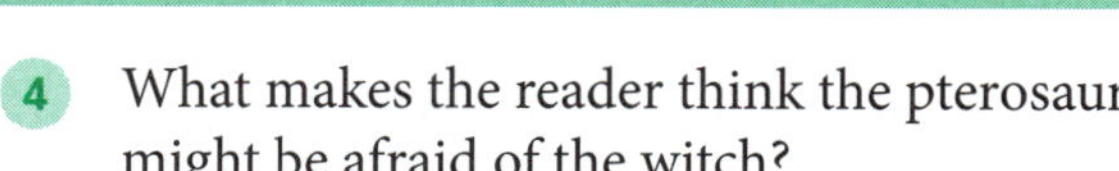

4 What makes the reader think the pterosaur might be afraid of the witch?

- **A** The pterosaur does not know where to get the berries.
- **B** Her name is the *Wicked Witch of the Ditch.*
- **C** His voice trembled when he said her name.
- **D** It's well known that witches eat pterosaurs.

5 What were Willa's *doubts*?

....

....

....

....

....

Answers and explanations on p. 99

Inferring questions

Use the **Step-by-step guide** on pages 40–43 to help you read the text and answer the **inferring** questions below. Circle the correct answers or write your answer on the lines.

Should you feed wild birds? (1)

There are a number of reasons why it is important not to feed wild birds.

Some foods, such as dry biscuits, can cause birds to choke. Salted or dry-roasted peanuts can be high in a natural toxin which poisons birds, even though it is harmless to humans. Milk can cause severe stomach upsets or even death. Margarines or vegetable oils on bread can damage birds' feathers. Damaged feathers can affect waterproofing, as well as a bird's ability to maintain body temperature and even to fly. None of this is worth the risk. Unless you know things like this you may cause birds to die when you feed them.

There are other problems you can cause when you feed wild birds. When natural food is short, birds may take food from feeding tables back to their chicks. If it is not suitable for the baby birds, they can choke. Birds also get used to a feeding routine and become dependent on you for food. If you are away for a time, they can become disoriented.

When feeding trays and bird baths aren't regularly cleaned, there is the danger of disease spreading. Many garden birds die each year from dirty bowls which breed parasites and bacteria.

I prefer my birds alive and flying about.

Marissa, Year Four

1. A natural toxin is something that
   - **A** makes food taste better.
   - **B** occurs naturally but can be harmful.
   - **C** adds a salty taste to food.
   - **D** is always deadly to humans.

2. Damaged feathers
   - **A** have serious consequences for birds.
   - **B** make birds look unattractive to humans.
   - **C** cause birds' colours to look dull to humans.
   - **D** are soon mended.

3. *None of this is worth the risk* implies that
   - **A** if you feed wild birds you risk harming them.
   - **B** it is wise to be a risk-taker.
   - **C** risk-taking is never a good idea.
   - **D** it is always worth feeding wild birds.

4. *When natural food is short* refers to food that
   - **A** you buy in shops.
   - **B** birds find for themselves from nature.
   - **C** is of a particular brand.
   - **D** is left out by humans.

5. Whose fault is it when birds die after eating from dirty bowls?
   - **A** birds who eat the mouldy food
   - **B** people who believe you should feed wild birds
   - **C** birds who haven't taken care of their health
   - **D** people who don't keep feeders clean

6. What does Marissa imply when she says that she prefers her birds alive?

   ....

   ....

   ....

   ....

Answers and explanations on pp. 99–100

Inferring questions

Use the **Step-by-step guide** on pages 40–43 to help you read the text and answer the **inferring** questions below. Circle the correct answers or write your answer on the lines.

My childhood memories

I remember:

- seeing the iceman deliver a block of ice to put in our icebox. He carried it on an old hessian sack balanced on his shoulder.
- feeling so hot that I had to lie on the bathroom tiles to cool down.
- my first tooth getting wobbly. Mum tied a cotton around it and tied the cotton to the doorknob. She banged the door shut but my tooth didn't come out. Later that day at lunchtime I chewed on something hard in my sandwich. It had come out by itself!
- finding my birthday presents hidden under my parents' bed. I tried to peek at them but then I heard someone coming down the hall. I hid in the wardrobe.
- watching my parents waltz around the living room to music coming from a record player. It had a needle and a turntable with a record on it that went round and round.

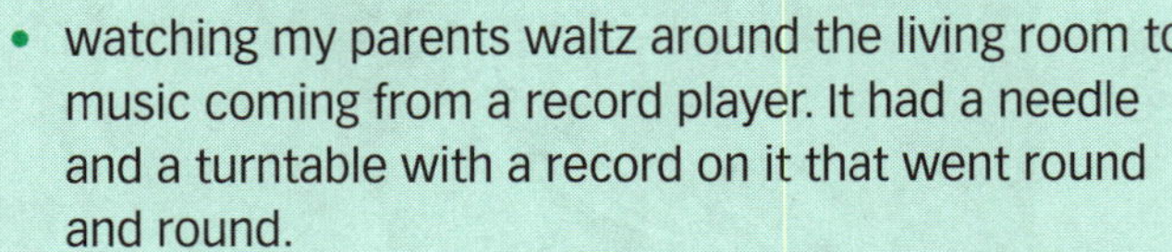

- playing with some baby pups at my Auntie's farm in the country and begging to be allowed to take one home. I named the one I loved Dinkly because his fur was dark and crinkly. I wasn't allowed to keep him.

by Sam

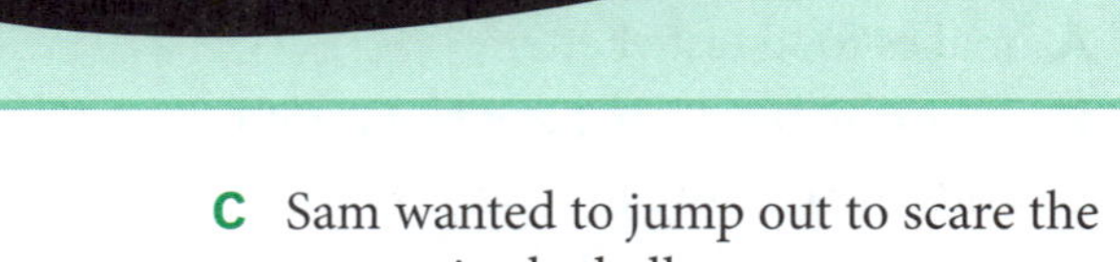

1. Why did Sam's family have an icebox? Choose all that apply.
   - **A** because they lived near the North Pole
   - **B** to help stop the ice from melting
   - **C** because they liked to put ice in their drinks when it was hot
   - **D** to keep their food cool so it didn't go bad

2. What was the hard thing in Sam's sandwich?
   - **A** a piece of broken lunch box
   - **B** a small piece of metal
   - **C** a tooth
   - **D** a nut in the sandwich filling

3. Why did Sam hide in the wardrobe? Choose all that apply.
   - **A** Sam felt guilty.
   - **B** Sam could hear better in the wardrobe.
   - **C** Sam wanted to jump out to scare the person in the hall.
   - **D** Sam did not want to be caught doing the wrong thing.

4. Sam is
   - **A** very young.
   - **B** over 50.
   - **C** female.
   - **D** male.

5. How did Sam feel about not being allowed to keep Dinkly?
   - **A** relieved
   - **B** disappointed
   - **C** satisfied
   - **D** glad

6. Name a piece of technology you can infer from the text that Sam did not have as a child.

   ....

Answers and explanations on p. 100

Inferring questions

Use the **Step-by-step guide** on pages 40–43 to help you read the text and answer the **inferring** questions below. Circle the correct answers or write your answer on the lines.

Should children have to earn their pocket money?

Transcript of a discussion from the TV program *Hello there, Australia*

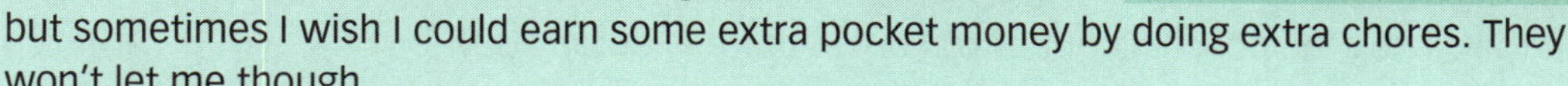

Celine: Thank you, Fourth Class, for taking part in our live discussion on *Hello there, Australia*. Our topic is: Should children have to earn their pocket money? Let's start with your view, Chilli.

Chilli: My parents won't let me earn pocket money. They give me my pocket money with no strings attached. I do have to do chores but they say that's because I'm part of the family and that it's only fair to share the work. I agree with that idea but sometimes I wish I could earn some extra pocket money by doing extra chores. They won't let me though.

Celine: Do others think pocket money with no strings is a good idea?

Connie: I think it's NOT a good idea. Just getting handouts doesn't teach you anything. In our family if we don't do our chores we don't get our pocket money. How else can you get five kids helping round the house?

Ricardo: I agree, Connie. And earning money teaches you things like saving up. The sooner we start earning, the better we'll be at dealing with money when we grow up.

Alice: But you can save up anyway. Not getting paid for doing your share teaches you money isn't as important as other things.

Celine: (turning to audience) Any questions?

1 What does Chilli think that is different from her parents' view?

- **A** She thinks pocket money should always be earned.
- **B** She thinks she should be allowed to do extra tasks for extra money.
- **C** She thinks pocket money should never be earned.
- **D** She thinks she should be allowed to do extra unpaid tasks.

2 Which child agrees exactly with what his or her parents think?

- **A** Chilli
- **B** Connie
- **C** Ricardo
- **D** Alice

3 What does Celine think about children earning pocket money?

- **A** She doesn't express any view on the topic.
- **B** She thinks pocket money with no strings is a good idea.
- **C** She believes in working hard for your pocket money.
- **D** She agrees with what Ricardo says.

4 What does Ricardo think about the idea of *pocket money with no strings*?

- **A** He thinks it is an excellent idea.
- **B** He thinks it is not a good idea.
- **C** He thinks it teaches you how hard it is to earn money.
- **D** He doesn't have any opinion about the idea.

5 What does Alice think about the idea of *pocket money with no strings*?

- **A** She thinks it is a terrible idea.
- **B** She mostly supports it.
- **C** She doesn't express any opinion about it.
- **D** She fully agrees with the idea.

6 What does *pocket money with no strings* mean?

....

....

....

....

Answers and explanations on pp. 100–101

Inferring questions

Use the **Step-by-step guide** on pages 40–43 to help you read the text and answer the **inferring** questions below. Circle the correct answers or write your answer on the lines.

Jim Jones at Botany Bay

... Our ship was high upon the seas when pirates came along,
But the soldiers on our convict ship were full five hundred strong;
They opened fire and so they drove that pirate ship away
But I'd rather joined that pirate ship than gone to Botany Bay.

With the storms a-raging round us, and the winds a-blowing gales
I'd rather drowned in misery than gone to New South Wales.
There's no time for mischief there, remember that, they say
Oh they'll flog the poaching out of you down there in Botany Bay.

Day and night in irons clad we like poor galley slaves
Will toil and toil our lives away to fill dishonored graves;
But by and by I'll slip m' chains and to the bush I'll go
And I'll join the brave bushrangers there, Jack Donahue and Co.

And some dark night all is right and quiet in the town,
I'll get the bastards one and all, I'll gun the floggers down.
I'll give them all a little treat, remember what I say
And they'll yet regret they sent Jim Jones in chains to Botany Bay.

From *Jim Jones at Botany Bay*, Anonymous, 1907

1. Why does Jim Jones say he'd prefer to be on the pirate ship than the ship he is on?
   - **A** He has always wanted to be a pirate.
   - **B** His ship is very uncomfortable in the high seas.
   - **C** He'd prefer the life of a pirate to that of a convict.
   - **D** The glamour of being a pirate has a strong attraction for him.

2. Why does Jim Jones say he'd prefer to drown than go to NSW?
   - **A** His seasickness is so bad that he'd rather drown than stay on the boat.
   - **B** The storms have made him miserable.
   - **C** He thinks he should be punished.
   - **D** He thinks drowning would be better than what awaits him in NSW.

3. Why will Jim Jones be *in irons clad*?
   - **A** As a convict he will be placed in iron chains to stop him escaping.
   - **B** As a bushranger he will wear iron armour.
   - **C** As a punishment he will be made to carry blocks of iron on his back.
   - **D** As a slave he can't afford any other clothing.

4. Jim describes bushrangers as *brave* because
   - **A** he has met Jack Donahue.
   - **B** he has met plenty of bushrangers.
   - **C** he wants to be a bushranger.
   - **D** he admires their freedom from authority.

5. What attitude does Jim Jones have towards the floggers in Botany Bay?

   ....

   ....

   ....

   ....

   ....

Answers and explanations on pp. 101–102

Inferring questions

Use the **Step-by-step guide** on pages 40–43 to help you read the text and answer the **inferring** questions below. Circle the correct answers or write your answer on the lines.

Alice in Wonderland

So she [Alice] was considering … whether the pleasure of making a daisy-chain would be worth the trouble of getting up and picking the daisies, when suddenly a White Rabbit with pink eyes ran close by her.

There was nothing so *very* remarkable in that; nor did Alice think it so *very* much out of the way to hear the Rabbit say to itself, 'Oh dear! Oh dear! I shall be late!' (when she thought it over afterwards, it occurred to her that she ought to have wondered at this, but at the time it all seemed quite natural); but when the Rabbit actually *took a watch out of its waistcoat-pocket*, and looked at it, and then hurried on, Alice started to her feet, for it flashed across her mind that she had never before seen a rabbit with either a waistcoat-pocket, or a watch to take out of it, and burning with curiosity, she ran across the field after it, and fortunately was just in time to see it pop down a large rabbit-hole under the hedge.

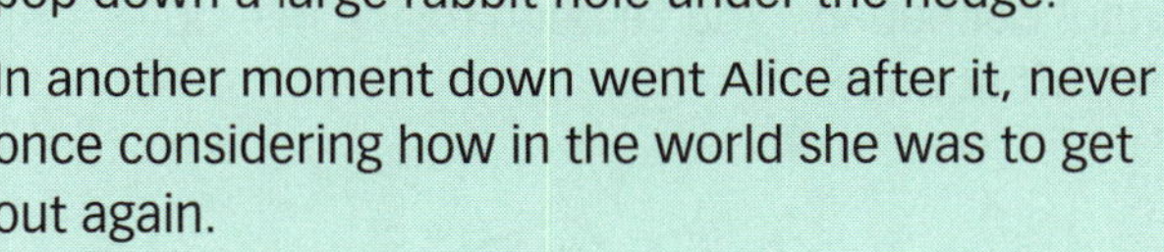

In another moment down went Alice after it, never once considering how in the world she was to get out again.

From *Alice in Wonderland* by Lewis Carroll, 1865

1. Why hasn't Alice begun to make a daisy chain?
   - **A** She is feeling too lazy to pick the daisies.
   - **B** She doesn't like picking daisies.
   - **C** She can't see any daisies.
   - **D** She can't decide whether the pleasure is worth the effort.

2. What amazed Alice when she first saw the White Rabbit?
   - **A** It took a watch out of its waistcoat-pocket.
   - **B** It ran past her.
   - **C** It was white with pink eyes.
   - **D** It stopped and stared hard at her.

3. Was the White Rabbit frightened by Alice?
   - **A** No, as she was not a very big girl.
   - **B** No, the White Rabbit was too worried about being late to notice her.
   - **C** No, because she sat very still.
   - **D** Yes, because the White Rabbit ran quickly past.

4. What made Alice burn with curiosity?
   - **A** She wanted to find out more about this very unusual rabbit.
   - **B** Her curiosity was making her hot and bothered.
   - **C** She was worried that her curiosity would kill the cat.
   - **D** She was keen to find it so she could ask it some questions.

5. Predict what might happen next from clues in the text.

   ....

   ....

   ....

   ....

   ....

Answers and explanations on p. 102

Step-by-step guide to **language** questions

Language questions involve examining how language is used in a text.

Use this **Step-by-step guide** to help you read the text and examine the way **language** is used to answer the questions below. Circle the correct answers or write your answer on the lines.

STEP 1 **Skim** the text to see what it is about and how it is organised.	**Read** the title, *When Jimbo Lost His Spots*. Look at the illustrations and other visual elements. Notice the body language of the two dalmations and what this suggests about them. Notice that there are quotation marks and exclamation marks included in the text. Make **predictions** about the subject and purpose of the text.
STEP 2 **Read** the text. **Monitor** your reading to make sure you understand the text.	**Visualise** and **connect** with the ideas in the text. **Think** about what you already know about the subject and the type of text, a narrative. Make **predictions.** Make **inferences**. Reflect on meanings and make **judgements**.

When Jimbo Lost His Spots

'Just look at you!' growled Jimbo's mother, a beautiful Dalmatian. 'You've been rolling in mud up to your ears. Go down to the river and wash it all off at once.'

Today was Easter Show Day so it was especially important that Jimbo looked handsome.

'But Muuum ...'

'At once,' barked his mother.

'Mothers!' Jimbo thought, plunging into the river. He rubbed his fur hard against some rocks on the river's edge. As he struggled back up the river bank, Sally, an old kookaburra, began to laugh loudly. 'You've washed off your spots,' she guffawed.

Jimbo swivelled his head around. No spots! Where had they gone? He'd be a laughing stock at the Easter Show. He daren't return to his mother in this state.

Suddenly, he remembered the face painters who had been at the Show last year. They'd help him. They'd paint his spots back on. Jimbo sped like an arrow to their stall at the Show.

Whew! He'd solved that problem. Now he wouldn't let down his family after all.

Question 1 **When his mother sees that Jimbo is muddy, how does she speak to him?**

A crossly　　B kindly　　C sweetly　　D loudly

STEP 3 **Read** the question. **Think** about what type of question it is. Work out what you need to do to answer it.	This is a **language** question. You need to examine the way language is used in the text to work out how Jimbo's mother speaks to him when she sees he is muddy.

STEP 4 **Think** about the text. Remember what you have read and **visualised**.

Scan the text to find the part that tells how Jimbo's mother speaks about his being muddy. Look at her choice of words and how they are said. Use your understanding to decide whether she speaks crossly, kindly, sweetly or loudly.

A is correct. Jimbo's mother exclaims '*Just look at you!*' when she sees Jimbo. Her exclamation shows she is surprised or shocked at the sight. The word *growled* is used to describe how she says the words, suggesting she is annoyed with him for getting mud *up to his ears*. Her next words are commands (*Go … wash it all off*) that she insists must be obeyed *at once*. These things combine to suggest that Jimbo's mother is cross with him.

Check the other options to confirm they are incorrect. **B** and **C** are words describing the opposite of how she speaks so they are incorrect. **D** may be true but the text doesn't use any words to suggest that she speaks loudly.

Question 2 The word *Muuum* is spelt that way because

A Jimbo is singing.
B Jimbo wants his mother to change her mind.
C the author can't spell.
D Jimbo loves the sound of the word.

STEP 3 **Read** the question. **Think** about what type of question it is. Work out what you need to do to answer it.

This is a **language** question. You need to examine how language is used in the text to work out why the word *Muuum* is spelt with three extra letter 'u's.

STEP 4 **Think** about the text. Remember what you have read and **visualised**.

Scan the text to find the part where Jimbo says the word *Muuum*. **Re-read** it to examine how the word is used in the context of the situation. Combine this with your own knowledge of sounds and spelling to help you work out why two extra letter 'u's are added to the spelling of the word.

B is correct. Jimbo says the word *'Muuum'* to try to make his mother change her mind. She has just told him to wash himself in the river '*at once*'. After he says '*But Muuum…*' she cuts him off and repeats '*At once*'. Jimbo used a whiny sort of voice, dragging out the word Mum to *Muuum*, to persuade her to let him off. The author adds the two extra letter 'u's to make the word sound the way Jimbo says it.

Check the other options to confirm they are incorrect. **A** and **C** are incorrect because there is no evidence in the text that Jimbo is singing or that he loves the sound of the name he uses. **D** is incorrect as it is unlikely the author could not spell the easy word Mum.

Question 3 Why is the word *Mothers* plural?

A There are several mothers in this story.
B Jimbo feels as if he has more than one mother.
C Plurals are always followed by an exclamation mark.
D Jimbo is exclaiming about how all mothers are the same.

STEP 3 **Read** the question. **Think** about what type of question it is. Work out what you need to do to answer it.

This is a **language** question. You need to examine how language is being used when Jimbo uses the plural word *Mothers*.

STEP 4 **Think** about the text. Remember what you have read and **visualised**.

Scan the text for the word *Mothers!* Re-read what comes before the word to find out what made Jimbo use the word in the plural. **Think** about why an exclamation mark is placed after the word.

D is correct. Jimbo says *Mothers* after he has been unable to persuade his mother to change her mind after she insists he wash himself in the river. He makes it an exclamation to express his feeling that all mothers are the same—they insist on their children staying clean.

Check the other options to confirm they are incorrect. **A** is incorrect as Jimbo's mother is the only mother in this story. **B** is incorrect as Jimbo doesn't feel he has more than one mother. He feels that mothers in general can be exasperating. **C** is untrue and is also not the reason that the word is plural.

Step-by-step guide to **language** questions *continued*

Language questions involve examining how language is used in a text.

When Jimbo Lost His Spots

'Just look at you!' growled Jimbo's mother, a beautiful Dalmatian. 'You've been rolling in mud up to your ears. Go down to the river and wash it all off at once.'

Today was Easter Show Day so it was especially important that Jimbo looked handsome.

'But Muuum ...'

'At once,' barked his mother.

'Mothers!' Jimbo thought, plunging into the river. He rubbed his fur hard against some rocks on the river's edge. As he struggled back up the river bank, Sally, an old kookaburra, began to laugh loudly. 'You've washed off your spots,' she guffawed.

Jimbo swivelled his head around. No spots! Where had they gone? He'd be a laughing stock at the Easter Show. He daren't return to his mother in this state.

Suddenly, he remembered the face painters who had been at the Show last year. They'd help him. They'd paint his spots back on. Jimbo sped like an arrow to their stall at the Show.

Whew! He'd solved that problem. Now he wouldn't let down his family after all.

Question 4 **Was Sally, the old kookaburra, laughing**

A with Jimbo?	B at the spots?	C with her partner?	D at Jimbo?

STEP 3 **Read** the question. **Think** about what type of question it is. Work out what you need to do to answer it.

- This is a **language** question. You need to examine the context in which Sally's laughter occurred—what caused her laughter and what she meant by it.

STEP 4 **Think** about the text. Remember what you have read and **visualised**.

- **Scan** the text to find the part about the kookaburra laughing. Re-read it to examine the **language** used to work out why she was laughing and how she laughed when she saw Jimbo come out of the river.

D is correct. Watching Jimbo's spots wash off and disappear is what made Sally, the kookaburra, laugh. The text says she *guffawed*, which means she laughed loudly and heartily. When she speaks she says '*You've washed off your spots*', showing that she is laughing AT what happened to him.

Check the other options to confirm they are incorrect. **A** is incorrect because Jimbo is not laughing so Sally can't be laughing WITH him. **B** is incorrect as the spots have disappeared so the kookaburra can't be laughing at them. The kookaburra doesn't have a partner in this story so **C** is also incorrect.

Question 5 The idiom (or saying) *a laughing stock* means

A something that can be sold.
B someone that laughs.
C someone everyone makes fun of.
D someone in trouble.

STEP 3	**Read** the question. **Think** about what type of question it is. Work out what you need to do to answer it.	This is a **language** question. You need to work out what *a laughing stock* means from how it is used in its context.
STEP 4	**Think** about the text. Remember what you have read and **visualised**.	**Scan** the text to find the part that has the words *laughing stock*. Re-read it to work out why Jimbo says these words and what they could mean in this context. Notice that the word *laughed* is also used earlier in the text. Check if that helps with understanding the meaning of this saying.

C is correct. Jimbo says he will be a *laughing stock at the Easter Show* after he finds he has lost his spots: *No spots! Where had they gone?* He sounds worried about being made a laughing stock. When Sally the kookaburra laughed she was guffawing AT what had happened to Jimbo. The answer that best matches these clues is that a laughing stock is someone that others will make fun of.

Check the other options to confirm they are incorrect. **A** is incorrect because there is nothing in the text that suggests Jimbo might be sold and he is not a thing. **B** is incorrect because Jimbo is being laughed at and not laughing himself. **D** is a possible meaning as Jimbo is in trouble, but it doesn't include the idea of being laughed at (i.e. *a laughing stock*).

Question 6 Why is Jimbo compared to an arrow?

Explain your answer on the lines below.

STEP 3	**Read** the question. **Think** about what type of question it is. Work out what you need to do to answer it.	This is a **language** question. You are being asked how the comparison used in the text suggests the similarity between two things—Jimbo and the arrow.
STEP 4	**Think** about the text. Remember what you have read and **visualised**.	**Scan** the text to find where the comparison (simile) is made: *Jimbo sped like an arrow to their stall at the Show.* **Think** about why Jimbo needs to get to the stall. Think about how an arrow flies to its target. Work out what makes Jimbo and the arrow alike.

Jimbo needs to get to the stall quickly so he can be back in time for the Easter Show. Arrows travel quickly and head straight towards their target. Jimbo's speed is compared to an arrow's because he is going straight towards the stall (his 'target') as quickly as he can.

Language questions

Use the **Step-by-step guide** on pages 52–55 to help you read the text and answer the **language** questions below. Circle the correct answers or write your answer on the lines.

Kwanza the white lion

Dear Diary

Dad took my sister and me to see a white lion in the zoo near Toowoomba today. His name is Kwanza and he has just had his first birthday.

Kwanza looks soft and cuddly. The zoo owner told us she handfed Kwanza when his mother stopped producing milk. She said he still loves his 'mum' and often tries to sit in her lap and suck her finger.

He also has a friend. You'll never guess what sort of friend. It is the zoo's dog, Honey. They like exploring, playing together and even wrestling.

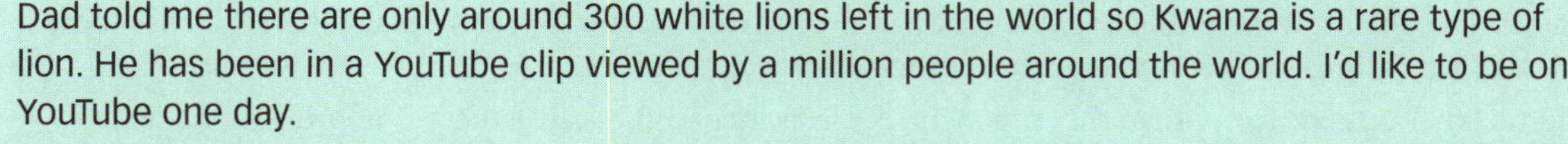

Dad told me there are only around 300 white lions left in the world so Kwanza is a rare type of lion. He has been in a YouTube clip viewed by a million people around the world. I'd like to be on YouTube one day.

When Millie heard that Kwanza had a special minced-meat birthday cake last year she asked if she could have one for her fourth birthday. You can guess the answer!

It was a fantabulous visit. I'm going to research white lions on the internet. I'll tell you what I find out tomorrow.

Benji

1. The words *soft and cuddly* are used in the text to
   - **A** give scientific information about the white lion.
   - **B** describe how the lion looks to Benji.
   - **C** remind the reader of a laundry commercial.
   - **D** give the zoo owner's description of the white lion.

2. Why is the word '*mum*' in inverted commas?
   - **A** The zoo owner is not talking about Kwanza's real mum.
   - **B** The zoo owner is a very important mum.
   - **C** The zoo owner is Kwanza's real mum.
   - **D** The zoo owner is talking about a mum she hasn't met.

3. Why does Benji say *even* wrestling?
   - **A** He is afraid the dog will hurt Kwanza.
   - **B** He is surprised that a lion and a dog could wrestle for fun.
   - **C** He uses it to mean 'also' in this context.
   - **D** He doubts that the lion and the dog wrestle.

4. How does Benji's use of the second person in his diary (e.g. *You'll never guess*) make him sound?
   - **A** friendly
   - **B** distant
   - **C** cold
   - **D** stuck up

5. What kind of word is *fantabulous*?
   - **A** French
   - **B** meaningless
   - **C** made by blending parts of words together
   - **D** very formal

6. How does Benji feel about his Diary?

....

....

....

....

Answers and explanations on pp. 102–103

Language questions

Use the **Step-by-step guide** on pages 52–55 to help you read the text and answer the **language** questions below. Circle the correct answers or write your answer on the lines.

Corroboree, Sydney

Transcript of a radio advertisement

Radio announcer: You're listening to singer-songwriter Casey Donovan, of the Gumbaynggir people, singing 'Listen With Your Heart' on Koori radio. You can catch her at Corroboree, Sydney, a celebration of the cultures of First Nations Australian peoples.

The first Corroboree, Sydney was documented by early explorers and held in the area currently known as Sydney's Royal Botanic Gardens. This ceremony is now honoured each year by a program of stunning events held at Bennelong Point, named after Bennelong of the Wangal people. He helped Captain Arthur Phillip learn the local language and traditions of the area back in the 1790s.

If you think Corroboree is for adults only, think again. Children can try the latest Aboriginal and Torres Strait Islander dance at Move it Mob Style, an interactive hip hop and dance show.

Or what about the Gurung parade where children carry their own handmade Waratah flowers to acknowledge local Eora culture?

There's something for everyone. Try listening to storytelling at the ghost story online archive project; or put away your hairbrush and microphone and join in singing Koori-oke.

Be there.

1. Which of these words adds a relaxed, casual tone to its sentence?
   - **A** documented
   - **B** held
   - **C** catch
   - **D** honoured

2. Which word could replace the word *documented* in this text?
   - **A** recorded
   - **B** heard
   - **C** performed
   - **D** viewed

3. Which word in paragraph 2 is included to persuade people to visit Corroboree, Sydney?
   - **A** first
   - **B** early
   - **C** stunning
   - **D** Royal

4. Which of the following is **not** the name of a First Nations Australian people?
   - **A** Gumbaynggir
   - **B** Bennelong
   - **C** Wangal
   - **D** Eora

5. The announcer says *think again* to
   - **A** emphasise the information that Corroboree, Sydney is also for children.
   - **B** make the listener feel ashamed.
   - **C** persuade the listener he or she is foolish.
   - **D** encourage the listener to bring more adults to Corroboree, Sydney.

6. How would the announcer say the closing words, *Be there*?

   ....

   ....

   ....

   ....

   ....

Answers and explanations on pp. 103–104

Language questions

Use the **Step-by-step guide** on pages 52–55 to help you read the text and answer the **language** questions below. Circle the correct answers or write your answer on the lines.

Newsflash: scientists find oldest living creature

Ming the Mollusc

When scientists found me
at the bottom of the seas
they brought me up and stored me
in the depths of a deep freeze.

I am a mollusc old and rare
older than they guessed.
I'd lived in seas for centuries.
It's true. I do not jest.

My shell did grow in layers.
One per year it's said.
They counted wrong, declaring
at four hundred I was dead.

They looked again and found
now that I was dead
I was not the age they'd thought me
I was 5 0 7 instead.

Born in fourteen ninety nine
I've seen a thing or four.
From Christopher Columbus
to Cook and many more.

The Guinness Book of Records
was quickly on the case.
Named me the oldest living thing
on earth, or any place.

Have I helped them learn new things?
Truth is I'm not certain.
But now that I'm a ghostly clam
I think I'll draw the curtain!

1. Who narrates the story of the poem?
   - **A** a scientist
   - **B** Ming the Mollusc
   - **C** a newspaper journalist
   - **D** the Guinness Book of Records

2. The main purpose of the poem is
   - **A** to raise concern about climate change.
   - **B** to persuade people to count more carefully.
   - **C** to amuse and entertain the reader.
   - **D** to prove scientists are dangerous.

3. Why does Ming say he'd seen *a thing or four* instead of *a thing or two*? Tick (✓) all that apply.
   - **A** He made a mistake. ....
   - **B** He needs *four* to rhyme with *more*. ....
   - **C** He is joking he's so old that he's seen twice as much as others. ....
   - **D** He has four eyes. ....

4. Where would you NOT find this poem? Choose all that apply.
   - **A** a children's newspaper
   - **B** a school magazine
   - **C** a scientific textbook
   - **D** a poetry collection

5. What is Ming's attitude to the scientists' research into molluscs?

   ....

   ....

   ....

   ....

Answers and explanations on p. 104

Language questions

Use the **Step-by-step guide** on pages 52–55 to help you read the text and answer the **language** questions below. Circle the correct answers or write your answer on the lines.

Night Noodle Markets

www.niftynoodlesatnight.com.au

Dreaming of some awesome family entertainment? The Night Noodle Markets could be just what you and your family are looking for.

Fragrant food. Delicious aromas to tease and tantalise as they waft by at the Night Noodle Markets.

Great locations. Outdoor dining at its best in the capital cities of Australia. Lap up the Asian hawker-style market atmosphere.

Take a peek at the menus on offer. Click on the cuisine of your choice below.

Chinese **Japanese** **Indian** **Malaysian** **Thai** **Vietnamese** **Singaporean**

When? The Night Noodle Markets kick off at 5 pm each evening, Monday to Saturday from November 9 to 26.

Where? Download a **MAP** to find a Night Noodle market in your capital city.

Supported by

Drinko Soft Drinks

Nifty Noodles

Local councils

1 What is *niftynoodlesatnight.com.au*?

A the owner's name
B a meaningless collection of letters
C the address of the website
D the name of the noodle markets

2 The language and images used on this website aim to be

A unusual. **B** enticing.
C off-putting. **D** formal.

3 The phrase *Fragrant food* appeals mainly to

A the sense of smell.
B the sense of hearing.
C the sense of touch.
D the sense of sight.

4 The expression *kick off* means

A conclude. **B** begin.
C draw to a close. **D** finish.

5 The word *cuisine* refers to

A a style of cooking characteristic of a particular place.
B Asian food.
C noodle dishes.
D night market food.

6 Why would the commands *Click on* and *Download* NOT be used in a newspaper advertisement for the Night Noodle Markets?

....

....

....

....

....

Answers and explanations on pp. 104–105

Language questions

Use the **Step-by-step guide** on pages 52–55 to help you read the text and answer the **language** questions below. Circle the correct answers or write your answer on the lines.

George Raper: a short life

George Raper was born in London in 1769, the third of six children. He began training as a captain's servant on the HMS *Rose* aged thirteen, the age young gentlemen joined the navy at that time.

In 1786 he was promoted to able seaman. He gained a place on the *Sirius* bound for Botany Bay. A paintbox of watercolours costing two month's salary was in his luggage. He spent two periods of around nine months in the new colony.

Later sea journeys took him to Capetown, Norfolk Island and the West Indies. He survived near starvation, shipwreck and hurricane. Promoted to lieutenant in 1795, he was given solo command of HMS *Expedition.* A year later, aged 27, he died from an unknown illness.

George Raper left behind maps, charts and paintings of plant and animal life from the places he visited. These are now important documents that tell of Australia's history.

An exciting footnote to George's story is the discovery of 56 unsigned watercolours of the flowers and birds of Sydney Cove. They had been kept as part of an 18th-century English earl's library. After proving them to be Raper's work, the National Library purchased them for the people of Australia.

1 The word *short* in the title of this text suggests that

- **A** George Raper was not very tall.
- **B** George Raper did not have a long life.
- **C** this is a brief account of George Raper's life.
- **D** George Raper went short of many things in his life.

2 The language used in this text is typical of

- **A** science reports.
- **B** newspaper stories.
- **C** letters to family or friends.
- **D** biographies.

3 What is an *able seaman*?

- **A** a young man who has turned 17
- **B** a rank above lieutenant in the navy
- **C** a young man who is very fit
- **D** a rank above captain's servant in the navy

4 The word *documents* is used in this text to refer to

- **A** accurate records.
- **B** handwritten accounts.
- **C** ideas.
- **D** men's and women's stories.

5 What does the term *bound* mean in *bound for Botany Bay*?

- **A** going to
- **B** tied to
- **C** linked with
- **D** moved in leaps and bounds

6 What does the term *footnote* mean in this text?

....

....

....

Answers and explanations on p. 105

Language questions

Use the **Step-by-step guide** on pages 52–55 to help you read the text and answer the **language** questions below. Circle the correct answers or write your answer on the lines.

The Third Hurdle

Willa was deep into the tunnel when she glimpsed a heavy stone door with the words Home of the Rainbow Dragon carved above it. She was close to the Rainbow Dragon's lair at last.

A plump creature, with remnants of lunch sprouting from his whiskers, catapulted out of nowhere and landed in front of her.

'RD's Guard here' he trumpeted, licking his chops with his hairy tongue. So here was her third hurdle.

'I am sorry to interrupt your lunch,' Willa said politely. 'You must be the Rainbow Dragon's most important guard?'

'Indeed,' he replied smugly.

'Does the Rainbow Dragon accept gifts?'

'Toads, bats, boiled boys. I accept … er, I mean, yes, he accepts that sort of thing.'

'Has he tried a beetle pancake?' Willa asked, whipping one from her backpack. 'It is said to give extraordinary powers to anyone who eats it.'

'Extraordinary powers, you say. Mmm. No problem.'

Smiling broadly, the guard plucked the pancake from Willa's outstretched palm and plopped it straight into his mouth. Within seconds, he was out cold on the floor.

Willa let out her breath—whe e e e w! She reached down and took the keys from the guard's belt. Third hurdle done and dusted!

From *The Rainbow Dragon* by Donna Gibbs

1. RD's Guard announces himself by
   - **A** whispering through his whiskers.
   - **B** loudly introducing himself by his title.
   - **C** giggling and snorting.
   - **D** using a singsong voice.

2. Why does Willa ask the guard if he is the Dragon's *most important* guard?
   - **A** She thinks he is the most important guard.
   - **B** She wants to sound friendly.
   - **C** She wants to flatter him so he'll listen to her.
   - **D** He is the Dragon's only guard.

3. What does the word *smugly* tell you about the guard's character?
   - **A** He is vain.
   - **B** He is ugly.
   - **C** He is happy to help.
   - **D** He is agreeable.

4. Why does the guard begin to say he accepts gifts ('*I accept …*') and then correct himself?
   - **A** He was really planning to take the gift for himself.
   - **B** His hairy tongue got caught in his whiskers.
   - **C** He has trouble with his words.
   - **D** He made the mistake on purpose.

5. The word *whe e e e w* is spelt with spaces
   - **A** to show there are really six separate words.
   - **B** to sound like Willa is slowly letting out her breath.
   - **C** to suggest Willa is stuttering from fear.
   - **D** because the typist made a mistake and it wasn't corrected.

6. What does the idiom *done and dusted* mean?

   ....

   ....

Answers and explanations on pp. 105–106

Language questions

Use the **Step-by-step guide** on pages 52–55 to help you read the text and answer the **language** questions below. Circle the correct answers or write your answer on the lines.

Words under the microscope

Over time, people have invented their language by using different ways to make up the words they need.

Myths and legends have given us names for days of the week and months of the year. Take *Tuesday*. It comes from the name Tiw, a Greek God. When a wolf monster threatened to destroy the Gods, Tiw bound him up with a chain made from the footsteps of a cat, the beard of a woman and the breath of a fish. The Anglo Saxons honoured his victory by naming a day of the week after him.

English borrows words from many other languages. Latin gave us the word *aborigine*. It comes from the latin *ab origine* meaning 'from the beginning'. The people who first settled in Latium, where Rome was later built, were called aborigines. Nowadays the word refers to the original inhabitants of a country anywhere in the world.

Sometimes words are made up from the first letters of several words, such as *Anzac* from Australia and New Zealand Army Corps. Or parts of words can be blended together. For example, the *sm* of the word *smoke* added to the *og* of the word *fog* makes *smog*. *Groaning* in a *mumble* is to *grumble*.

What about emailing, blogging and googling? Meaningless words? Your great-great-grandparents would have thought so.

1. The idiom *under the microscope* in the title means
   - **A** looked at on the screen of your computer.
   - **B** looked at closely.
   - **C** put under a microscope in a laboratory.
   - **D** looked at as an enlarged copy.

2. The expression *Take* Tuesday is
   - **A** relaxed and conversational.
   - **B** uptight and formal.
   - **C** impolite and rude.
   - **D** ungrammatical and silly.

3. The words *footsteps of a cat, the beard of a woman and the breath of a fish* name
   - **A** things that can't be held.
   - **B** real objects that can be held.
   - **C** imaginary objects that can't be seen.
   - **D** items you'd find in a shopping trolley.

4. Blending words involves
   - **A** adding a prefix to a whole word.
   - **B** adding whole words together.
   - **C** mixing letters up.
   - **D** combining parts of words.

5. Why would your great-great-grandparents think the words *emailing*, *blogging* and *googling* were meaningless?

   ....

   ....

   ....

   ....

   ....

   ....

Answers and explanations on pp. 106–107

Language questions

Use the **Step-by-step guide** on pages 52–55 to help you read the text and answer the **language** questions below. Circle the correct answers or write your answer on the lines.

The seahorse

Text 1: The seahorse's lament

I've lost my little brothers and some of my sisters. When the storm came their tails lost their grip on the seaweed and were swept away by the current. I know I will never see them ever again. I'm so hungry too. I hope more plankton drift my way. I can't wait to slurp them up through my snout. Maybe that will cheer me up.

Text 2: Unusual features of the seahorse

A seahorse is a fish with a horse-like head. It has a crown of spines that varies in design from one seahorse to another, just as thumbprints on humans vary. Each of its eyes moves on its own. The most unusual fact of all is that the fathers gives birth to the babies. After a courtship in which the seahorses link tails, dance with each other, swim in circles and even change colours, the female lays eggs through a tube into an opening in the male's pouch. When the baby seahorses are ready to be born, the male relaxes his pouch muscle and pumps them out into the sea.

1. The title of Text 1 is *The seahorse's lament*. What is a lament?
   - **A** a poem
   - **B** a conversation
   - **C** a debate
   - **D** a sad tale

2. Text 1 is told
   - **A** in the first person.
   - **B** in the second person.
   - **C** in the third person.
   - **D** without any particular voice.

3. Which word in Text 1 suggests that the seahorse has some doubts about what he says?
   - **A** can't
   - **B** never
   - **C** so
   - **D** Maybe

4. Text 2 is told
   - **A** in the first person.
   - **B** in the second person.
   - **C** in the third person.
   - **D** without any particular voice.

5. The language of Text 2 is mainly
   - **A** informative.
   - **B** imaginative.
   - **C** reflective.
   - **D** persuasive.

6. Use information from the two texts to label the parts of the seahorse.

Answers and explanations on p. 107

Step-by-step guide to **judgement** questions

Judgement questions involve making judgements.

Use this **Step-by-step guide** to help you read the text and make **judgements** to answer the questions below. Circle the correct answers or write your answers on the lines.

STEP 1 **Skim** the text to see what it is about and how it is organised.	**Read** the title, *Peter Pan*. Look at the illustration and other visual elements. Notice the facial expressions and body language of the man and woman in the picture. You can **predict** that they are characters in the text. Notice the text is in paragraphs. Make **predictions** about the subject and purpose of the text.
STEP 2 **Read** through the text. Make sure you understand it.	**Visualise** and **connect** with the ideas in the text**. Think** about what you already know about the subject and the type of text, a narrative. Make **predictions**. Make **inferences**. Reflect on meanings and make **judgements**.

Peter Pan

All children, except one, grow up. They soon know that they will grow up, and the way Wendy knew was this. One day when she was two years old she was playing in a garden, and she plucked another flower and ran with it to her mother. I suppose she must have looked rather delightful, for Mrs. Darling put her hand to her heart and cried, 'Oh, why can't you remain like this forever!' This was all that passed between them on the subject, but henceforth Wendy knew that she must grow up. You always know after you are two …

Wendy came first, then John, then Michael.

For a week or two after Wendy came it was doubtful whether they would be able to keep her, as she was another mouth to feed. Mr. Darling was frightfully proud of her, but he was very honourable, and he sat on the edge of Mrs. Darling's bed, holding her hand and calculating expenses, while she looked at him imploringly.

From *Peter Pan* by JM Barrie, 1911

Question 1 **Who tells the story?**

A Wendy **B** Mrs. Darling **C** Mr. Darling **D** a narrator

STEP 3 **Read** the question. **Think** about what type of question it is. Work out what you need to do to answer it.	This is a **judgement** question. You need to make a judgement about evidence from the text, and from your understanding of narrative and voice (first, second and third person), to work out who is telling the story.

STEP 4 **Think** about the text. Remember what you have read and **visualised**.

Look for evidence in the text that tells who is telling the story—whether it is the voice of Wendy, Mrs. Darling, Mr. Darling or a narrator. Consider the evidence to make a **judgement**.

D is correct. The story is told in the third person. You can tell from the way it is told that the person speaking knows all about the characters. This means it is a narrator's voice, not a character's voice.

Check the other options to confirm why they are incorrect. **A, B** and **C** are incorrect. The characters do not tell the story but are part of it. The comments made by these characters are reported, and commented on, by the narrator rather than taking place at the time.

Question 2 ***All children, except one, grow up.*** **This sentence captures the reader's interest because**

A it is about children.
B it is a short sentence.
C it makes readers want to know more about the one who doesn't grow up.
D it is about growing up.

STEP 3 **Read** the question. **Think** about what type of question it is. Work out what you need to do to answer it.

This is a **judgement** question. You need to work out what best explains why the sentence captures the reader's interest.

STEP 4 **Think** about the text. Remember what you have read and **visualised**.

Scan the text to find and re-read the sentence. Look at where the sentence is placed and how it is said. **Think** about what you predict the story will be about when you read it.

C is correct. The sentence begins the narrative and is said in a confident way as if the speaker has some interesting things to reveal to the reader. It suggests that the story will be about someone unusual—someone who doesn't grow up in the way other children do. This is intriguing and makes the reader want to find out more.

Check the other options to confirm why they are incorrect. **A** is incorrect because the sentence is not so much about children as about the one child who does not grow up. **B** is incorrect because while it describes the sentence accurately, it is the idea it expresses that captures interest. **D** is incorrect because it is the idea of a child not growing up that stands out dramatically in the sentence.

Question 3 **You can judge that the Darling family is**

A not rich. B rich. C foolish. D wicked.

STEP 3 **Read** the question. **Think** about what type of question it is. Work out what you need to do to answer it.

This is a **judgement** question. You need to look for clues in the way the Darling family lives, how they behave and what they talk about to make a judgement.

STEP 4 **Think** about the text. Remember what you have read and **visualised**.

Re-read the whole text. Look for clues that tell you whether the family is not rich, rich, foolish or wicked. Consider the evidence to make a **judgement**.

A is correct. You read that Mr. Darling is considering not keeping his daughter because *she was another mouth to feed* even though both he and his wife want to keep her. This shows that the family is not rich.

Check the other options to confirm why they are incorrect. **B** is incorrect because there is evidence of the family not having enough money for food. **C** is incorrect because there is no evidence that the family has done anything foolish. **D** is incorrect because Mr. Darling is described as *honourable* so he would not behave in a wicked way.

Step-by-step guide to **judgement** questions *continued*

Judgement questions involve making judgements.

Peter Pan

All children, except one, grow up. They soon know that they will grow up, and the way Wendy knew was this. One day when she was two years old she was playing in a garden, and she plucked another flower and ran with it to her mother. I suppose she must have looked rather delightful, for Mrs. Darling put her hand to her heart and cried, 'Oh, why can't you remain like this forever!' This was all that passed between them on the subject, but henceforth Wendy knew that she must grow up. You always know after you are two …

Wendy came first, then John, then Michael.

For a week or two after Wendy came it was doubtful whether they would be able to keep her, as she was another mouth to feed. Mr. Darling was frightfully proud of her, but he was very honourable, and he sat on the edge of Mrs. Darling's bed, holding her hand and calculating expenses, while she looked at him imploringly.

From *Peter Pan* by JM Barrie, 1911

Question 4 **Mrs. Darling puts *her hand to her heart* because**

A she is waving away a fly.
B she thinks her strong feelings come from there.
C she thinks Wendy should care more for her mother's heart.
D she has a sudden pain in it.

STEP 3	**Read** the question. **Think** about what type of question it is. Work out what you need to do to answer it.	This is a **judgement** question. You need to make a judgement about the reason Mrs. Darling puts her hand on her heart from evidence in the text.
STEP 4	**Think** about the text. Remember what you have read and **visualised**.	**Scan** the text to find and re-read the part where it says Mrs. Darling puts her hand to her heart. **Think** about when she does this and what causes her to do it. Consider the evidence to make a **judgement**.

B is correct. Mrs. Darling puts *her hand on her heart* just after she has admired little Wendy bringing her a flower. Then she touches her heart while saying she wishes Wendy could stay as she is forever. You can judge this is because she thinks the tug between pleasure and pain that makes her cry out is taking place in her heart.

Check the other options to confirm why they are incorrect. **A** is incorrect as there is no mention of flies in the text. **C** is incorrect as there is no evidence that she blames Wendy for anything. **D** is incorrect because the pain in her heart is not a physical pain.

Question 5 What do you predict Mr. Darling will do?

A decide not to keep Wendy
B make the breakfast
C talk sternly to Mrs. Darling
D conclude they must keep Wendy

STEP 3	**Read** the question. **Think** about what type of question it is. Work out what you need to do to answer it.	This is a **judgement** question. Use evidence from the text to **predict** what Mr. Darling is likely to do.
STEP 4	**Think** about the text. Remember what you have read and **visualised**.	Re-read the whole text. **Think** about what kind of person Mr. Darling is and how he feels about and treats his family. Consider the evidence to make a **judgement**.

D is the most likely. Mr. Darling is described as *honourable* and someone who wants to do the right thing. He is proud of his daughter and caring towards his wife. He holds her hand for comfort and would find it hard to refuse her begging him (*looked imploringly at him*) to keep their daughter.

Check the other options to confirm why they are incorrect. It is possible Mr. Darling would decide not to keep Wendy (**A**) but less likely for the reasons given above. **B** is incorrect as Mr. Darling's concern is deep so he is unlikely to be thinking about his next meal just then. **C** is incorrect because his attitude towards Mrs. Darling is very loving and considerate. He may speak this way on occasion but it is unlikely he would talk sternly to her at this point in the story.

Question 6 What evidence in the text shows the story was written a long time ago?

Explain how you came to your conclusion.

....

....

....

....

STEP 3	**Read** the question. **Think** about what type of question it is. Work out what you need to do to answer it.	This is a **judgement** question. You need to make a judgement about what evidence suggests the story was written a long time ago.
STEP 4	**Think** about the text. Remember what you have read and **visualised**.	Re-read the text looking for evidence that shows the story was written a long time ago. **Think** about what you already know about the story of *Peter Pan*.

Evidence that would lead you to think the story was written a long time ago includes:

- the old-fashioned language, such as *rather delightful*, *henceforth* and *honourable*
- the formal use of the parents' names, Mrs. Darling and Mr. Darling, which is not common in modern stories
- the date the text was written, 1911, which is over 100 years ago.

The title, *Peter Pan*, is the name of a story that everyone—young and old—seems to know. This might be another reason for thinking that the story has been around for a very long time.

Judgement questions

Use the **Step-by-step guide** on pages 64–67 to help you read the text and answer the **judgement** questions below. Circle the correct answers or write your answer on the lines.

The day I disappeared

I vividly remember the day I disappeared. One minute I was standing there with my friends and the next I was gone. Well, I wasn't gone exactly. I was still there. But no-one could see me.

'Where's Scotty?' I heard Bill ask.

'Don't ask me,' Jo replied. 'He was here a minute ago.'

'I'm here,' I said.

'Let's go to the cafe anyway,' said Bill. 'He must have had to leave all of a sudden.'

'Look at me,' I shouted. 'I'm right beside you.'

'Yep. Let's go. I'm starving,' said Jo.

'I'm hungry too,' I said miserably.

I walked with them to the cafe feeling very peculiar. Jo ordered but she didn't order for me.

'One beef burger,' I said to the salesperson. I sat down at a table by myself and waited. And waited. And waited. OK. I really was invisible. I decided to go home.

'I'm home, Mum,' I called. I could hear the shower running. She mustn't have heard me. I took my bag upstairs. Red, my cocker spaniel, was on my bed. She bristled and growled as I came into the room.

'Good dog, Red,' I said. Well, at least she knew I was there. Even if no-one else did!

1 Who narrates this story?

A Bill
B Scotty
C Jo
D Mum

2 How do Scotty's friends react to his disappearance?

A with very little concern
B with alarm
C with fear
D by making a fuss

3 Why does Scotty sit at a table by himself and not with his friends?

A The waitress will be able to bring his hamburger to him there.
B He wants to eat his hamburger by himself.
C He feels afraid of his friends.
D He realises his friends still can't see him.

4 What kind of story is *The day I disappeared*?

A realistic
B fantasy
C science fiction
D historical fiction

5 How does the narrator react to his own disappearance?

....

....

....

....

....

....

Answers and explanations on pp. 107–108

Judgement questions

Use the **Step-by-step guide** on pages 64–67 to help you read the text and answer the **judgement** questions below. Circle the correct answers or write your answer on the lines.

The advantages and disadvantages of the internet

Transcript of a conversation

Silver: Mum says I spend far too much time on the internet but I don't think I do. You can do so many different things on it.

Tim: I agree. In fact, it saves time. You can find out things you want to know in seconds.

Christa: The whole family finds it useful at our house. Mum and Dad shop online, we watch movies and my sister plays games nonstop. Even Gran does crosswords on the internet.

Silver: You forget time when you're on the net.

Paddy: But that can be a problem. My parents say it stops me doing things I should be doing. It probably does, but I really like it. And it's made lessons at school much more fun.

Therese: That's for sure. Mum says it makes it too easy for her boss to send her work when she's off duty. That's a disadvantage.

Kara: And there's cyberbullying. That's a big disadvantage.

Tim: There's always been bullying though. And the internet even has good programs that teach you how to handle things like that. I don't think any of us would like to be without it now, would we?

1 Whose family approves of spending time on the internet?

A Silver's **B** Therese's
C Paddy's **D** Christa's

2 Whose parents have very similar opinions about time spent on the internet?

A Paddy and Silver's
B Therese and Kara's
C Tim and Christa's
D Kara and Paddy's

3 What is Paddy's reaction to his parents' views about the internet?

A He strongly disagrees with what they think.
B He feels angry with them for thinking as they do.
C He partly agrees with their view.
D He thinks they don't see its educational value.

4 Who uses the most arguments to support the use of the internet?

A Christa **B** Tim
C Paddy **D** Silver

5 How accurate is Tim's view that none of the group would like to be without the internet?

....
....
....
....
....
....
....
....

Answers and explanations on p. 108

Judgement questions

Use the **Step-by-step guide** on pages 64–67 to help you read the text and answer the **judgement** questions below. Circle the correct answers or write your answer on the lines.

Camouflage in the animal kingdom

Camouflage is a form of disguise. Animals use camouflage as a means of survival.

The most common form of camouflage for an animal is to blend into its environment. For example, sharks and dolphins have greyish-blue colouring that blends well with the colour of water. Similarly, geckoes or lizards have developed brownish grey colours that blend with the earth. Foxes and hares in the arctic region go a step further. They grow a brown coat for summer and a white coat for winter.

A zebra's wavy black stripes merge into the wavy lines of tall grasses. The difference in colour isn't a problem as the zebra's main enemy, the lion, is colourblind. The spotted coat of a leopard also blends well with the dappled shadows of leaves and sunlight. Leopards like to lie along a tree trunk ready to pounce on their prey.

The Australian sea dragon looks just like a bunch of tangled seaweed. Stick insects stay motionless on twigs for long periods of time and are indistinguishable from their hosts. Reef stonefish look the same as the lumps of rocky coral that surround them. Step on one of these 'stones' by mistake and you discover they *can* be deadly. This is the law of the jungle at work.

1 This text would be suitable for inclusion in

- **A** a book about animals and their environments.
- **B** a newspaper article about scientific discoveries.
- **C** a book of short stories.
- **D** a young child's picture book about animals.

2 What is similar about the way sharks and geckoes use their colouring?

- **A** They can frighten predators with their colours.
- **B** They are both dark grey in colour so they can be easily overlooked.
- **C** They blend into the colours of their environments to avoid danger.
- **D** There are no similarities.

3 What is the main benefit of animal camouflage?

- **A** It makes animals easier to recognise.
- **B** It draws attention to animal behaviour.
- **C** It helps conceal animals from predators.
- **D** It alerts animals to predators.

4 Which of these is NOT a useful camouflage method?

- **A** shedding fur of one colour and growing a coat of another
- **B** blending into your surroundings
- **C** looking similar to something in your environment
- **D** hunting your prey

5 What could an animal do to stay undetected when it looks like its surroundings?

- **A** imitate the behaviour of its surroundings
- **B** strike out when touched
- **C** disturb its surroundings
- **D** repeatedly change its colour

6 What attitude does the author have towards the *law of the jungle*?

....

....

....

....

....

Answers and explanations on pp. 108–109

Judgement questions

Use the **Step-by-step guide** on pages 64–67 to help you read the text and answer the **judgement** questions below. Circle the correct answers or write your answer on the lines.

The clockwork insect

Human beings thought they invented gears. New research shows that nature got in there first.

Have a look at this diagram of the tops of a planthopper's legs, an insect around the size of a flea, to see for yourself.

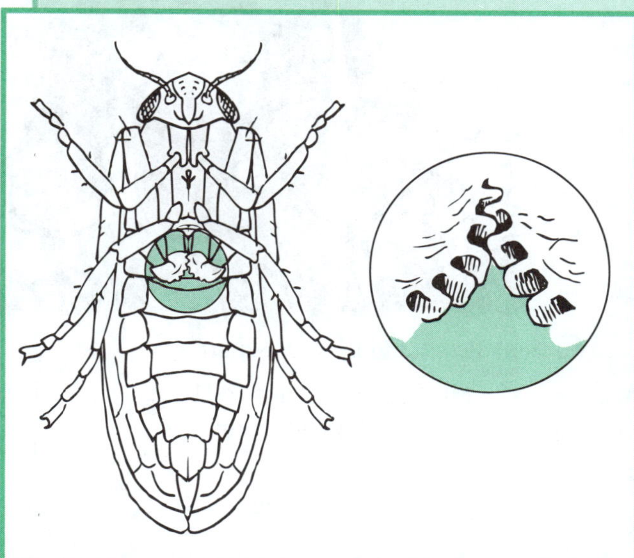

On the top of each leg, where the hind legs join its body, you can see a row of small interlocking teeth. When a planthopper jumps these teeth make its legs rotate and extend at the same time. They work like gears!

Scientists in the UK studied the insects' movements using a high-speed camera with a microscope attached. They put the insects on their backs and tickled their tummies to make them kick. They found their hind legs could move within a millionth of a second of each other. Their legs being connected by the gears helps them to jump faster and further.

The teeth of most modern gears are shaped similarly to those used in the 18th century, when a mathematician designed shapes that could be easily cut by the machines they had available. Now high-precision machines, such as 3D printing machines, will make it possible to create tiny gears similar to those found on young planthoppers. We are learning …

1 What is so surprising about the discovery of gears on planthoppers?

- **A** They work very well.
- **B** They are extremely tiny.
- **C** Their teeth interlock smoothly.
- **D** Humans thought they had invented gears.

2 Where would you be most likely to read a text of this kind?

- **A** in a school newsletter
- **B** in a comic book
- **C** in a newspaper article
- **D** in a Wikipedia entry

3 What is the author's attitude to the news of this discovery?

- **A** enthusiastic
- **B** disappointed
- **C** unenthusiastic
- **D** concerned

4 The author includes a diagram of the planthopper's legs to

- **A** give visual evidence of their interlocking teeth that work like gears.
- **B** show the distance a planthopper can jump.
- **C** make the article look better.
- **D** point out what a lifesize planthopper looks like.

5 What is the most important thing scientists have learned from the discovery of the planthopper's gears?

....

....

....

....

....

Answers and explanations on p. 109

Judgement questions

Use the **Step-by-step guide** on pages 64–67 to help you read the text and answer the **judgement** questions below. Circle the correct answers or write your answer on the lines.

Anthony Browne's *King Kong*

Edgar: My favourite book is Anthony Browne's *King Kong.*

Cooper: I didn't like it much. It's so over the top.

Edgar: There is a pile of action but that makes it exciting.

Cooper: I agree with you there. But you can't believe any of it—not the dinosaur battle, too many rescues and escapes, and not that mad bit on top of the Empire State Building at the end.

Edgar: But it's like a fairytale. You're not meant to believe it in the way you're saying. And that bit at the end is the best part. It's not just any old ape up there. It's King Kong. He might have done beastly things but he's so brave and gentle. Then humans shoot bullets at him!

Cooper: Well they had to rescue Ann somehow. Did you think he should have escaped?

Edgar: Of course not. You feel sad and mixed up about it all. But that's why I like the book so much. The illustrations are brilliant at making you feel everything at once.

Cooper: I did rather like the movie.

Edgar: Which version? The original movie from 1933?

Cooper: Don't know. Don't think so. Naomi Watts was in it.

Edgar: That's the 1994 one. Mmmm.

1. In discussing Anthony Browne's *King Kong* Edgar and Cooper
   - **A** mostly agree with each other.
   - **B** mostly disagree with each other.
   - **C** have a few similar opinions.
   - **D** never agree on anything.

2. If Cooper were to write a review of Browne's *King Kong* it would be
   - **A** quite favourable.
   - **B** of mixed opinion.
   - **C** fairly critical.
   - **D** strongly favourable.

3. Edgar's point of view about the book is convincing because
   - **A** it is different from Cooper's point of view.
   - **B** he uses evidence from the book to support his opinions.
   - **C** he likes the book a great deal.
   - **D** he talks more than Cooper does.

4. The discussion about the movie, *King Kong*, reveals that
   - **A** Cooper has seen the 1933 version.
   - **B** Edgar is well informed about the movies.
   - **C** Cooper is not a good judge of movies.
   - **D** Edgar likes to show off.

5. Make a judgement about the way Cooper presented his point of view.

   ....

   ....

   ....

   ....

Answers and explanations on p. 110

Judgement questions

Use the **Step-by-step guide** on pages 64–67 to help you read the text and answer the **judgement** questions below. Circle the correct answers or write your answer on the lines.

The Rainbow Dragon's Lair

To her surprise, the cave-like room Willa entered that morning was empty except for lots of bats hanging from the roof, a wooden treasure chest, and what looked like a beautifully coloured patchwork quilt lying against the wall of the cave. So far so good.

As she knelt to look more closely at the treasure chest, a roar echoed around the room. Willa stayed stock still, petrified. The quilt had moved. It had become a snarling, spitting, roaring dragon, ready for the kill.

Scenes from her past life rolled across the screen of Willa's mind. The faces of her family looked imploringly at her. They'd starve to death if she didn't get their fortune back. She had to find a way to survive the dragon and recapture the treasure.

With no tricks or cunning left to help her, Willa would have to use her grandfather's charm. Well, it'd better work or she was breakfast! Drawing on all her courage, Willa recited the words:

Dragons are red
Dragons are blue
When you tickle their toes
They'll be kinder to you.

She somersaulted across the room, tickling the dragon's toes as she catapulted past. The Dragon paused and a strange look came over its face. Willa stared into its eyes and waited.

From *The Rainbow Dragon* by Donna Gibbs

1. This text is part of
   - **A** an interview between a girl and a dragon.
   - **B** a nonfiction account of dragon behaviour.
   - **C** a story about a girl and a dragon.
   - **D** a well-known fairy tale.

2. The atmosphere created in paragraph two is
   - **A** amusing.
   - **B** relaxed.
   - **C** dreamy.
   - **D** dramatic.

3. Which description does NOT apply to the Rainbow Dragon?
   - **A** It likes to sleep in the day.
   - **B** It is good natured.
   - **C** It has a terrible roar.
   - **D** It has stolen from others.

4. Willa's actions are
   - **A** brave and determined.
   - **B** cowardly and weak.
   - **C** desperate and evil.
   - **D** wise and confident.

5. How likely is it that Willa will escape with the treasure? Use evidence from the text to support your answer.

....

....

....

....

....

....

Answers and explanations on pp. 110–111

Judgement questions

Use the **Step-by-step guide** on pages 64–67 to help you read the text and answer the **judgement** questions below. Circle the correct answers or write your answer on the lines.

That it is a waste of money to develop robots

I think there are several reasons that suggest developing robots is wasted money. In San Diego recently $325 000 dollars of taxpayers' money was spent on inventing a robotic squirrel. The research proved that squirrels are able to frighten off predators by wagging their tails. Do you need a robotic squirrel to work this out?

What about AIBO, a robotic pet, developed in Japan? In Japanese *aibou* means 'pal' or 'buddy'. These pets have been developed at huge expense mainly to provide entertainment. They've been used in movies and music videos. Universities have used them for educational purposes (e.g. Robocup). But in 2006 they were discontinued in order to make the company more profitable. Was it worth the huge investment?

Then there's NAO, the robot companion developed by a French company. Its main purpose is to make life better for humans. It speaks 19 languages and has its own personality. It can tell children a story, help in the classroom or the home, or act as a companion to those who need one. A fully operational one costs $16 000. Is that value for money? Who can afford it anyway?

There may be good reasons I haven't thought of why it's worth developing robots but so far I'm unconvinced.

Kent Promo, Burke West Primary

1. What is the purpose of Kent's question at the end of paragraph 1?
   - **A** to criticise the research
   - **B** to question if a robotic squirrel would be helpful
   - **C** to convince himself robotic squirrels are necessary
   - **D** to show he knows less than the researchers

2. Which sentence could be used as an argument for developing robots?
   - **A** In Japanese *aibou* means 'pal' or 'buddy'.
   - **B** These have been developed at huge expense mainly to provide entertainment.
   - **C** Was it worth the huge investment?
   - **D** Universities have used them for educational purposes.

3. Which of these statements could NOT be used to argue against Kent's views?
   - **A** Robots can save costs when used as receptionists, security personnel, hospital workers and guides.
   - **B** Research into robots helps us better understand how the brain works.
   - **C** Robots can do jobs that are dangerous for people to do.
   - **D** Developing robots is not cost effective.

4. Which statement is NOT true of the argument Kent presents?
   - **A** Kent selects examples to support his point of view.
   - **B** Kent uses language persuasively.
   - **C** Kent makes up some 'facts' to support his point of view.
   - **D** Kent's argument builds towards a conclusion.

5. How convincing is Kent's view that it is wasteful to spend money on developing robots? Explain.

   ....

   ....

   ....

   ....

   ....

Answers and explanations on p. 111

Judgement questions

Use the **Step-by-step guide** on pages 64–67 to help you read the text and answer the **judgement** questions below. Circle the correct answers or write your answer on the lines.

Botany Bay Herald

Could it have happened?

For a very long time, many people have thought Willem Janszoon's voyage to Australia on the Dutch ship, the *Duykfen*, in 1606, was the first recorded sea journey from Europe. Now some people are wondering if a Portuguese ship reached Australia before that date.

The discovery of a small image of a kangaroo (*canguru* in Portuguese) is what makes them ask this question. The roo is painted on a Portuguese document dated from between 1580 and 1620. It is pictured curled inside a large capital D on the page of a book containing words and music for hymns for religious ceremonies.

Where did the artist learn what the kangaroo, a native animal of Australia, looked like? If it really is an Aussie roo, and not a badly drawn deer or some other similar animal, then the Portuguese may have visited Australia *before* 1606. There are no records of such journeys but that's not surprising. The Portuguese were secretive about their trade routes and a fire in Lisbon in 1755 destroyed many of the records they'd kept.

If it is proven the Portuguese got to Australia before the Dutch, then there'll be some new information for our history books. That's nothing new though—it happens all the time.

1. You can tell this is a newspaper article rather than a history text book because
   - **A** words like *Dutch* and *Portuguese* are used.
   - **B** the language is very formal.
   - **C** the language is mainly informal.
   - **D** it includes ideas and opinions.

2. In the headline *it* refers to the idea that
   - **A** the Dutch came to Australia after the English.
   - **B** the English came to Australia before the Portuguese.
   - **C** the Portuguese came to Australia before the Dutch.
   - **D** the Dutch came to Australia before the Portuguese.

3. There is some doubt that the image is a kangaroo because
   - **A** the drawing is hard to see clearly.
   - **B** it could be an animal similar to a kangaroo.
   - **C** kangaroos all look the same.
   - **D** the word *kangaroo* is *canguru* in Portuguese.

4. Could the discovery of the picture of the roo help to rewrite history?
   - **A** certainly
   - **B** definitely not
   - **C** definitely
   - **D** possibly

5. What does the last sentence suggest about history?

   ....

   ....

   ....

   ....

   ....

   ....

Answers and explanations on pp. 111–112

BRINGING IT ALL TOGETHER

Mixed questions

Use the **Step-by-step guide** on page 4 to help you read the text and answer the questions below. Circle the correct answers or write your answer on the lines.

How is glass made?

The process of making glass in ancient cultures may have been learned from what happens naturally to sand when a volcano erupts. The very high heat of the lava melts the sand and forms a hard, glassy substance called obsidian.

Today glass is made by mixing large quantities of sand with sodium ash and limestone. When sodium ash and limestone are added to sand they lower its melting point. If the aim is to make coloured glass then minerals such as cobalt or sulphur are added.

The ingredients are put into a furnace and heated to around 1700 °C (3092 °F), a temperature that is hotter than molten lava. The mixture blends into a syrupy mass which becomes liquid glass. Those who work with the mixture wear protective clothing including goggles, hoods and long thick gloves.

While the liquid glass is still hot, air is blown into it through a long pipe. In this way, glassblowers are able to shape the material. They form glass bottles, drinking glasses, jewellery and myriad other things. It is also used to make optical fibres for use in medicine and as parts for modern communication systems. Glass is eco-friendly in that it is endlessly 100% recyclable.

1. When a volcano erupts the lava turns sand
   - **A** into earth.
   - **B** into more sand.
   - **C** into a glassy substance.
   - **D** into lava.
2. Sodium ash and limestone are added to sand
   - **A** to lower its melting point.
   - **B** to double its quantity.
   - **C** to make coloured glass.
   - **D** to raise its melting point.
3. The brackets around (*3092 °F*) mean that the temperature is
   - **A** hotter than 1700 °C.
   - **B** cooler than 1700 °C.
   - **C** the same as 1700 °C.
   - **D** twice as hot as 1700 °C.
4. Protective clothing is worn by workers
   - **A** to keep in the heat.
   - **B** to protect the furnace.
   - **C** to warn others to keep away from them.
   - **D** to protect their bodies from the high heat.
5. *They form … myriad other things.* The word *myriad* means
   - **A** a few.
   - **B** many.
   - **C** trillions.
   - **D** one or two.
6. What does *endlessly 100% recyclable* mean?

   ....

   ....

   ....

Answers and explanations on p. 112

Mixed questions

Use the **Step-by-step guide** on page 4 to help you read the text and answer the questions below. Circle the correct answers or write your answer on the lines.

Ratty times

Mrs Rat: Have you seen Harold?

Mr Rat: He said he was going to sunbathe up on deck, dear.

Mrs Rat: That boy will be the end of me. He's a lazy good-for-nothing. He should be in chains along with the convicts in their cells.

Mr Rat: Now, dear. No need to be harsh.

Mrs Rat: Well, Arthur, I feel cross. I'm so tired and hungry.

Mr Rat: (*sounding wistful*) Me too. It's over 240 days since we left Portsmouth. I counted the marks on the wall in one of the cells. Our last decent meal was when we docked at Cape Town on the 13th October, 1787.

Mrs Rat: (*her voice rising shrilly*) And not only that. I've had to make a new nest from scratch as the skipper ordered the old one cleaned away. The cheek! That's where our new litter was sleeping. And where was their big brother? Off gallivanting about the ship.

Unseen female convict: Help! Help! (*A piercing screech shatters the air.)*

Mrs Rat: Ah, thank goodness. Frightening the ladies as usual. Tell him he's needed here, will you Mr Rat. I'm at the end of my tether with all these newborns.

1 Mrs Rat's son is named

- **A** Cape Town.
- **B** Arthur.
- **C** Mr Rat.
- **D** Harold.

2 The stage directions used here give instructions about

- **A** how the characters should move on the stage.
- **B** the way the characters should say their lines.
- **C** how the lighting should be placed.
- **D** when the characters should say their lines.

3 How are the characters of Mr and Mrs Rat different?

- **A** She is calm while he is irritable.
- **B** She is irritable while he is even tempered.
- **C** He is calm while she is easy going.
- **D** He is unkind while she is irritable.

4 Why does Mrs Rat say *Ah, thank goodness*?

- **A** She likes to hear convicts in distress.
- **B** Mr Rat passes her a lump of cheese.
- **C** Screeches are music to her ears.
- **D** She knows Harold must be nearby.

5 The author writes about rats as though

- **A** they deserve everyone's respect.
- **B** they are to be despised.
- **C** they have many human qualities.
- **D** they need to stand up for their rights.

6 Can you work out where Mr and Mrs Rat's ship was heading from what you learn about their voyage? Use evidence from the text to support your answer.

....

....

....

....

Answers and explanations on pp. 112–113

Mixed questions

Use the **Step-by-step guide** on page 4 to help you read the text and answer the questions below. Circle the correct answers or write your answer on the lines.

Woollarawarre Bennelong (c.1764–1813)

Woollarawarre Bennelong grew up near the Parramatta river where he learned to gather oysters, catch fish with a *muting* (spear) and make a *nawi* (canoe) from stringy bark. He was a respected member of the Wangal people.

In 1788 Governor Arthur Philip had two First Nations men kidnapped so he could learn more about First Australians. One of them escaped; the other was Bennelong. He lived for a time in an upstairs room in Governor Philip's house, bringing his wife, Barangaroo, to visit. Later he chose to live in a brick hut built for him by Governor Philip at Bennelong Point (*Jubgalee*), a well-known gathering place for the Eora people, and where the Opera House now stands.

Source: Wikimedia Commons

Bennelong learned English and became a useful interpreter and go-between for Governor Philip and the local Indigenous people. In 1792 he sailed to England with Governor Philip and was received by King George III. He returned to Sydney on HMS *Reliance* in 1795 in poor health. He was badly affected by homesickness, the cold climate, a dependence on alcohol and long delayed travel plans.

Back in the colony, he found himself no longer fully accepted by either the white or black communities. He was killed in a tribal fight in 1813 and buried at Kissing Point on the banks of the Parramatta River.

1 What is a *muting*?

A an oyster **B** a spear
C a fish **D** a canoe

2 Which word written in italics in the text is the odd one out?

A *muting* **B** *nawi*
C *Jubgalee* **D** *Reliance*

3 Why is there a c. before Bennelong's birth date but not his death date?

c. stands for the Latin word *circa* meaning 'about'.

A His birth date isn't certain but his death date is.
B His birth date is an important date.
C The author couldn't find the correct date for his birth.
D The author wants to draw attention to his birth date.

4 Why does Bennelong Point have this name?

A Bennelong asked that it be given that name.
B There is a restaurant of that name in the Opera House.
C The Eora name was hard to pronounce.
D It was named after Bennelong.

5 The main purpose of this text is to

A describe a problem faced by Governor Philip.
B give information about First Australians' way of life.
C give an overview of Bennelong's life.
D describe the English way of life.

6 How did Bennelong's relationship with Governor Philip change over time? Use evidence from the text to support your view.

....

....

....

....

Answers and explanations on pp. 113–114

Mixed questions

Use the **Step-by-step guide** on page 4 to help you read the text and answer the questions below. Circle the correct answers or write your answer on the lines.

The Wonderful Wizard of Oz

From the far north they heard a low wail of the wind, and Uncle Henry and Dorothy could see where the long grass bowed in waves before the coming storm …

Suddenly Uncle Henry stood up.

'There's a cyclone coming, Em,' he called to his wife. 'I'll go look after the stock.' Then he ran toward the sheds where the cows and horses were kept.

Aunt Em dropped her work and came to the door. One glance told her of the danger close at hand.

'Quick, Dorothy!' she screamed. 'Run for the cellar!'

Toto jumped out of Dorothy's arms and hid under the bed, and the girl started to get him. Aunt Em, badly frightened, threw open the trap door in the floor and climbed down the ladder into the small, dark hole. Dorothy caught Toto at last and started to follow her aunt. When she was halfway across the room there came a great shriek from the wind, and the house shook so hard that she lost her footing and sat down suddenly upon the floor.

Then a strange thing happened.

The house whirled around two or three times and rose slowly through the air. Dorothy felt as if she were going up in a balloon.

From *The Wonderful Wizard of Oz* by L Frank Baum, 1900

1 Who or what made the wailing sound heard by Dorothy and Uncle Henry?

A Aunt Em **B** Toto
C the wind **D** the grass

2 Why does the long grass *bow*?

A It is welcoming the storm.
B The wind is forcing the grass to bend downwards.
C The wind is pushing the grass in all directions.
D The wind makes the grass stand upright.

3 In what way is Dorothy's reaction like Uncle Henry's?

A They both complain about what is happening.
B They both avoid their responsibilities.
C They both decide to hide.
D They both show concern for others rather than for themselves.

4 Why does only Aunt Em hide in the cellar?

A She is the only one who knew about it.
B The others chose different hiding places.
C Toto gets lost and the others have to look for him.
D She is the only one who has time to get there.

5 The most suitable title for this text would be

A The cyclone.
B Toto gets lost.
C Dorothy goes up in a balloon.
D Danger ahead.

6 How does the atmosphere change after Dorothy loses her footing? Use evidence from the text to support your answer.

....

....

....

....

....

....

Answers and explanations on p. 114

Mixed questions

Use the **Step-by-step guide** on page 4 to help you read the text and answer the questions below. Circle the correct answers or write your answer on the lines.

Talking about books

Gazz: Have you read *Charlie and the Chocolate Factory*?

Fabiano: No. Want some grapes? What's it like?

Gazz: Thanks, Fab. Well, the main character's Charlie Bucket. He gets very excited when he wins a ticket to tour a chocolate factory because he's from this penniless family. The other four kids who win tickets are all revolting. You'd love the drawings. They're great.

Fabiano: Are they those drawings that look as if they're scribbled in a hurry but get the feeling just right?

Gazz: That's them. It's Quentin Blake. I did a project on him at school last year.

Fabiano: His drawings in *James and the Giant Peach* really suit the story. My dad used to read that to me when I was younger. I've read it lots of times.

Gazz: These grapes are great. Would I like it?

Fabiano: I think you would. It gets you in because after his parents are killed by a rhino, James has to live with his two cruel aunts, Sponge and Spiker.

Gazz: Whew! Does a real rhino kill him?

Fabiano: Well, real in the story. James ends up living in the peach with some weirdo friends.

Gazz: Sounds good.

1. Fabiano and Gazz are eating
   - **A** nuts.
   - **B** chocolate.
   - **C** peaches.
   - **D** grapes.

2. This conversation is
   - **A** a formal classroom discussion.
   - **B** a casual conversation.
   - **C** an interview.
   - **D** a talk show on radio.

3. Both of the books talked about include characters who
   - **A** live with their parents.
   - **B** are named Quentin.
   - **C** are very nasty.
   - **D** are without parents.

4. The boys' attitude to Blake's drawings is
   - **A** admiring.
   - **B** envious.
   - **C** unimpressed.
   - **D** disrespectful.

5. When Fabiano says *It gets you in* he means that the story
   - **A** makes you want to give up reading.
   - **B** makes you want to read indoors.
   - **C** tricks and deceives you.
   - **D** captures your interest.

6. Do you think Gazz would be likely to read *James and the Giant Peach*? Use evidence from the text to support your answer.

   ....

   ....

   ....

   ....

   ....

   ....

Answers and explanations on pp. 114–115

Mixed questions

Use the **Step-by-step guide** on page 4 to help you read the text and answer the questions below. Circle the correct answers or write your answer on the lines.

The age of discovery

Columbus discovered the 'new world' of the Americas on an expedition sponsored by the Spanish in 1492. The indigenous peoples that inhabited the Americas were made up of many distinct nations and tribes. In 1522 Magellan led a successful sailing expedition around the world. His journeys proved to Europeans that the world was not flat and there was still much to be discovered.

From the 16th to the 18th centuries, the Spanish, Portuguese, French, Dutch, Scandinavian and English competed with each other to expand their empires. They fought over better trading routes and founded colonies to add to their wealth and power.

Some historians argue that Spanish, Portuguese and French ships may have reached Australia as early as the 16th century. Dutch and British expeditions certainly reached Australia in the 17th century.

Reports of Australia sent back by the navigators to their homelands usually described its land and its peoples as uninhabitable and uninteresting. In 1623, for example, a Dutch captain, Jan Carstensz, described the north of Australia as 'the most barren and arid region on earth' and its people as wretched and poor.

James Cook, whose voyage to Australia in the 1780s led to the British colonisation of this country, took a different view. He praised the fertility of the Botany Bay area and said of the First Australians that 'in reality they are far happier than we Europeans'.

1 In which year did Magellan successfully sail around the world?

A 1492 **B** 1522 **C** 1780 **D** 1623

2 Magellan's voyage proved that

- **A** Australia was a long way from Europe.
- **B** the world was not flat.
- **C** Columbus was a better sailor than Magellan.
- **D** Magellan was a better sailor than Columbus.

3 The 'new world' was new to

- **A** the indigenous people of the Americas.
- **B** Columbus and other Europeans.
- **C** those who lived there already.
- **D** nobody at all.

4 An alternative title for this text could be

- **A** Columbus and Magellan.
- **B** Captain Cook gives Australia a good report card.
- **C** European colonisation from the 16th to the 18th century.
- **D** European colonisation from the 10th to the 12th century.

5 Whose view of events is not considered in the text?

- **A** the Spanish rulers
- **B** the map makers
- **C** the indigenous peoples
- **D** the Dutch navigators

6 Why did Carstenz and Cook reach such different conclusions about Australia and its peoples? Use evidence from the text to support your view.

Answers and explanations on p. 115

Mixed questions

Use the **Step-by-step guide** on page 4 to help you read the text and answer the questions below. Circle the correct answers or write your answer on the lines.

Should you feed wild birds? (2)

I disagree with my classmate, Marissa, who argues that you shouldn't feed wild birds. Having wild birds visit your garden is such a pleasure. It's much better than having birds in cages!

Providing food can be a help to birds when food is short. During the breeding season extra food can mean the survival of the birds' babies.

It is important, though, to follow these rules:

1 Keep food and water dishes clean. Wash after every feed to avoid spreading disease.
2 Check what your local council says about feeding wildlife.
3 Plant native flowering trees for birds that eat nectar and birds that eat insects that eat nectar.
4 Find out what food is best for the kind of birds who visit. This might be very small pieces of apple or wild birdseed mix. Do not feed them sugar, honey, bread or processed foods.
5 Follow a feeding routine so birds become used to it. Arrange for someone to take over if you are away for a longish time.
6 Make sure feeding places are where predators will have difficulty in reaching the birds.

Some research shows that native bird numbers have increased in many places around the world thanks to humans leaving food for them.

I say go for it!

Felix, Year 4

1 The main purpose of this text is to
- **A** describe the pleasures of feeding wild birds.
- **B** argue it is not harmful to feed wild birds if you are careful.
- **C** discuss different points of view about feeding wild birds.
- **D** discuss current research into feeding wild birds.

2 Felix disapproves of
- **A** following a feeding routine.
- **B** feeding wild birds.
- **C** birds in cages.
- **D** research into bird life.

3 Which food should you NOT feed wild birds? Choose all that apply.
- **A** processed foods
- **B** sugar
- **C** honey and bread
- **D** birdseed mix

4 Which of these statements does NOT support the feeding of wild birds?
- **A** In harsh times it can provide food for their babies.
- **B** It gives pleasure to humans.
- **C** It can provide birds with a balanced diet.
- **D** It can help birds become entirely dependent on humans for food.

5 The word *it* in the expression *go for it* means
- **A** leave carefully chosen food out for the birds.
- **B** visit places where the bird population has increased.
- **C** do more research into whether feeding birds is harmful.
- **D** follow your own feelings.

6 Does Felix show that he cares about the environment? Use information from the text to support your answer.

....

....

....

....

Answers and explanations on pp. 115–116

Mixed questions

Use the **Step-by-step guide** on page 4 to help you read the text and answer the questions below. Circle the correct answers or write your answer on the lines.

My trip to China

Dear Little Sis

Thanks for your email with the news from home. I didn't know you were learning Mandarin at school! My travels have brought me to Beijing so I am hearing lots of Mandarin spoken. I was lucky to arrive here just *after* a sandstorm. My host told me sandstorms come from the northern deserts and are troublesome for people and the environment.

I'm just back from seeing the Great Wall of China. It's like a long dragon winding its way through the landscape. We were told it goes for about 8800 km. Some parts are in ruins as they are over 2000 years old.

My next ambition is to travel to Hangzhou so I can visit the themed islands on Thousand Island Lake (千島湖). I'm hoping to see Bird Island and Monkey Island, but most of all the Island to Remind You of Your Childhood. When you're older, Little Sis ... :)

Amazingly there are cities under this manmade lake. In 1959 the government 'drowned' them so they could build a dam and reservoir. One of the ancient lost cities was rediscovered recently by divers. You could google it to find some photos if you like.

Until next time

love
Theo

1 Which places has Theo NOT visited? Choose all that apply.

A Beijing
B Hangzhou
C the Great Wall of China
D Island to Remind You of Your Childhood

2 Theo's host thinks sandstorms are troublesome because

A they are a risk to people's health and destroy farmlands.
B they come from the north.
C they are a nuisance.
D they should be prevented.

3 Theo compares the Great Wall of China to

A a monkey. **B** a pathway.
C a dragon. **D** a ruins.

4 Theo's attitude towards his little sister is

A distant. **B** bossy.
C scratchy. **D** affectionate.

5 What does *the government 'drowned' them* mean in the text?

A The cities were taken over by the government.
B The government flooded the cities so that they were underwater.
C The cities died a natural death.
D The cities were moved by the government to another district.

6 In what ways does Theo use the internet? Use evidence from the text to support your answer.

....

....

....

....

....

Answers and explanations on pp. 116–117

Mixed questions

Use the **Step-by-step guide** on page 4 to help you read the text and answer the questions below. Circle the correct answers or write your answer on the lines.

The Ugly Animal Preservation Society

Ben: Have you heard of the Ugly Animal Preservation Society?

Chloe: No. What's that?

Ben: It's a group who want people to know more about animals who get neglected because of how they look.

Chloe: Hey, that's a great idea. You mean animals that look ugly who might become an endangered species?

Ben: Exactly. They had a competition at the British Science Festival recently to choose the world's ugliest animal.

Chloe: Which animal won?

Ben: It was the blobfish. They've made it a mascot for the society.

Chloe: I've never heard of a blobfish.

Ben: That proves the point! They live in the deep sea off the coast of Australia where fishing trawlers catch them in their nets by mistake.

Chloe: That's a shame. Are they really, really ugly?

Ben: Well, they have no muscle so they look all rubbery and gross.

Chloe: Which other animals did well?

Ben: There was a heavy, slow-moving flightless parrot. And a proboscis monkey that has a very long nose and a pot belly.

Chloe: I vote we start a branch of the society.

Ben: Yes! Let's set up a blog and invite all our friends to choose an animal for *our* mascot!

Chloe: You're on.

1 Which animal won the world's ugliest animal competition?

A the blobfish
B the koala
C the flightless parrot
D the proboscis monkey

2 Ben and Chloe's attitude towards the Ugly Animal Preservation Society is

A unfriendly. **B** disapproving.
C enthusiastic. **D** uninterested.

3 The blobfish is a good mascot because

A it is rubbery and without muscle.
B it is hard to find in the depths of the sea.
C it has a sad expression on its face.
D it is a symbol of animals that are neglected because they are 'ugly'.

4 Which of the following occurred first in time?

A Ben and Chloe set up a blog.
B The blobfish wins first place in the competition.
C A competition to choose the world's ugliest animal is held.
D The Ugly Animal Preservation society is formed.

5 Chloe's slang expression, *You're on*, means

A that she is keen to work with Ben on his idea.
B that Ben should write up the blog.
C that Chloe thinks Ben's idea is not worth doing.
D that Ben can be part of their society.

6 Do you judge the blobfish to be an unfortunate animal?

....

....

....

....

Answers and explanations on p. 117

Mixed questions

Use the **Step-by-step guide** on page 4 to help you read the text and answer the questions below. Circle the correct answers or write your answer on the lines.

Barangaroo

Barangaroo (?–1791) grew up fishing and hunting in an area near Port Jackson that had been occupied by the Cammeraygal nation for thousands of years. She was a woman of strong character, well known for her courage and individuality.

As the second wife of Bennelong, Barangaroo could have lived in Governor Philip's house when Bennelong was there as an adviser on First Nations customs and language. She chose to stay with her own people instead. She did dine with the English party quite often but she refused to wear clothes or drink the wine she was offered. On special occasions she wore a bone painted with white clay through her nose, something usually worn by males rather than females.

Later she lived with Bennelong in a hut built for him by Governor Philip. Their only daughter, Dilboong (*Bellbird*), died when she was just a few months old. Barangaroo died in 1791 not long after her daughter's death. Bennelong cremated her body, with her fishing basket beside her, on a funeral pyre at a ceremony held in Governor Philip's garden in Sydney Cove.

In 2006 a new 22-hectare development near Sydney's Darling Harbour was named Barangaroo, in her memory, by popular vote.

1 Which nation was Barangaroo from?

A Bennelong
B Dilboong
C Wangal
D Cammeraygal

2 Why did Barangaroo not live at the home of Governor Philip?

A The Governor wouldn't have her there.
B Bennelong asked her not to live there.
C She preferred to live with her own people.
D Her people would not allow her to live there.

3 Why is Barangaroo's birth date recorded as a question mark?

A Her birth certificate has been lost.
B Her birth date is not known or recorded anywhere.
C It was written too unclearly for the typist to copy.
D She asked for it to be left out.

4 Which of these statements that give extra information about Barangaroo is likely to be untrue?

A She had two spear wounds on her body.
B She threatened a man with a big stick because she thought he was cruel.
C She liked to shop for fashionable clothes.
D She broke a spear belonging to Bennelong in a fit of anger.

5 *She was a woman of strong character*

Does the text provide evidence that supports this view of Barangaroo? Explain your answer.

....

....

....

....

....

Answers and explanations on pp. 117–118

Mixed questions

Use the **Step-by-step guide** on page 4 to help you read the text and answer the questions below. Circle the correct answers or write your answer on the lines.

Marianne Musgrove's *The Worry Tree*

The Worry Tree is a chapter book suitable for children from 8 to 12. It tells the story of ten-year-old Juliet, who is a collector of strange things and a worrywart. She worries about everything you can think of including problems with things that concern most boys and girls—family relationships, friendships, coping with change and bullying.

All is not gloom, however. Ophelia (nicknamed Oaf) provides plenty of comic relief as Juliet's annoying little sister. She does things such as hide in the wardrobe to spy on Juliet and time how long she spends in the toilet! The rest of the family, including her Nana, can be pretty peculiar at times.

When Juliet gets a bedroom to herself in the family home she discovers a Worry Tree painted on the wall beneath some peeling wallpaper. Juliet learns that the animals on its branches are there to hold her worries while she sleeps. Petronella the pig is good for school worries, for example. There's even a hollow in the tree where Juliet can put her can't-think-what-sort-of-worries.

Juliet learns to use the tree as a way of thinking about how to deal with the things that make her life difficult. Strong characters, plenty of humour and real problems brought to life by lively writing make this a must read.

1. What is the first name of the author of *The Worry Tree*?
   - **A** Petronella
   - **B** Juliet
   - **C** Marianne
   - **D** Ophelia
2. A *worrywart* is
   - **A** someone who worries about everything all the time.
   - **B** something that grows on your skin.
   - **C** someone who has hives.
   - **D** someone with a severe illness.
3. What is the main purpose of the text?
   - **A** to tell the story of the book
   - **B** to describe the characters
   - **C** to advertise the book
   - **D** to review the book
4. The Worry Tree is
   - **A** a real tree.
   - **B** an imaginary tree.
   - **C** a painting of a tree.
   - **D** a photo of a tree.
5. The author of the text
   - **A** strongly recommends the book.
   - **B** criticises the book.
   - **C** suggests boys won't like the book.
   - **D** has mixed feelings about the book.
6. Would you find a Worry Tree useful? Explain.

   ....

   ....

   ....

   ....

   ....

   ....

   ....

Answers and explanations on p. 118

Mixed questions

Use the **Step-by-step guide** on page 4 to help you read the text and answer the questions below. Circle the correct answers or write your answer on the lines.

New Year's resolutions

Dear Diary

Happy New Year.

You think I'm going to tell you my New Year's resolutions now, don't you?

Well, I'm not going to but I am going to tell you the ones I think my family should make. I'm telling you, dear diary, because I don't think I'd better tell them.

1. Mum: She should promise to always make my brother stay in his room for hours and hours when he annoys me.
2. Dad: He should promise to stop correcting my pronunciation. It is very embarrassing.
3. My brother: He should promise never to annoy me ever, ever again.
4. The baby: He should promise to get better table manners and not throw his porridge on the wall so we have to clean it up.
5. My big sister: She should promise never again to say she's better than I am at football and cricket. I know she isn't though I haven't told her that.
6. Aunt Jessica: She should promise to stop taking photos. I don't like having to smile all the time and mum nudges me if I don't.
7. Ms Jenkins. Ms Jenkins should promise not to find such a lot of spelling mistakes in my stories.

Danny

1 Danny treats his diary as though it were
- **A** someone from whom he keeps secrets.
- **B** a close friend in whom he can confide.
- **C** his brother.
- **D** Aunt Jessica.

2 How is Ms Jenkins different from the others in Danny's list?
- **A** She is female.
- **B** She knows Danny.
- **C** She is not part of the family.
- **D** She points out mistakes made by Danny.

3 Why does Danny repeat the word *hours*?
- **A** He wants to annoy his brother.
- **B** He's emphasising that his mother shouldn't waste time.
- **C** He's emphasising he'd like his brother kept away for a very long time.
- **D** He wants to annoy his mother.

4 Which family member will NOT make the resolution Danny suggests for them?
- **A** his big sister
- **B** his dad
- **C** his aunt
- **D** his baby brother

5 Danny hasn't told his big sister he's better at football and cricket than she is because
- **A** Aunt Jessica told him not to tell her.
- **B** she wouldn't believe him.
- **C** he doesn't think he is.
- **D** his sister is a bully.

6 Which resolution do you judge would be the most important to Danny? Explain your reasons.

....

....

....

....

Answers and explanations on pp. 118–119

Mixed questions

Use the **Step-by-step guide** on page 4 to help you read the text and answer the questions below. Circle the correct answers or write your answer on the lines.

Come to the Alice

US: Want a family holiday in the middle of a red sand desert that stretches for hundreds of kilometres in all directions?

YOU: No thanks.

US: Think again. Have the holiday of a lifetime when you come to the Alice, set in the heart of history.

YOU: But there'll be nothing for the kids to do.

US: Think again. There are activities for the whole family. You can:

- bike ride to a gap in the McDonnell Ranges where there are rock wallabies and a beautiful waterhole
- sail in a hot-air balloon over swaying spinifex grasses
- swim in ancient waterholes and tropical pools set in stunning landscapes
- listen to fascinating Dreamtime legends
- visit Uluru where you can ride a camel at dawn around this sacred monolith
- learn about the area's first inhabitants, the Western Arrernte people, who've lived in the Central Australian desert for thousands of years, and, if you time it right, you can
- watch the annual 'sailing and rowing' regatta held on a dry riverbed in bathtubs on legs with pirate ships firing flour bombs.

YOU: Thanks, mate. No worries. Tell the Alice we're on our way.

1 The main purpose of this text is to persuade families to

A visit Uluru.
B change their minds.
C visit the Alice.
D think about holiday activities.

2 The text mainly targets

A young children.
B families.
C teenagers.
D adults.

3 The activities promoted by the text are

A typical everyday activities.
B adventurous and unusual activities.
C a mixture of physical activities.
D the same old things offered by all holiday resorts.

4 The words used to describe the landscape make it sound

A inviting and attractive.
B arid and bare.
C ancient and worn out.
D rugged and challenging.

5 Why is the Alice described as *set in the heart of history*?

A It is in the centre of Australia.
B It is where First Nations people have lived for thousands of years.
C You can learn about its history at the tourist centre.
D It is a great place to visit.

6 The YOU in the text speaks three times. What do his or her spoken words suggest about this person?

....

....

....

....

....

....

Answers and explanations on p. 119

Mixed questions

Use the **Step-by-step guide** on page 4 to help you read the text and answer the questions below. Circle the correct answers or write your answer on the lines.

Idioms

All languages have their own idioms and it has been estimated that English has over 25 000 expressions of this kind. Idioms enrich the language and give it its own special character. Idioms often sound quite humorous if you think about their literal meanings. Here are some English examples:

- *to cost an arm and a leg* means something is very expensive.
- *to keep your eyes peeled* means you are on the alert.
- *raining cats and dogs* means it is raining very heavily.

You can see that you can't work out the meanings of these idioms from knowing what each individual word means in the group. What these groups of words literally mean doesn't make much sense. People don't pay for things with an arm and a leg; nobody peels their eyes; and cats and dogs don't fall from the sky when it rains. When you recognise that these are idioms, you think about what they mean quite differently.

Imagine you grow up speaking a language such as Cantonese, Japanese or Greek. Then your family moves to Australia and you have to learn to speak and understand English. You carefully build up your vocabulary and then you hear a word you know, only to discover it doesn't mean what it usually means. This can make learning a new language very puzzling.

1 How many idioms does English contain?

A more than 25 000
B less than 25 000
C exactly 25 000
D no-one has tried to count

2 In the text, the phrase *each individual word* means

A all words together.
B each word by itself.
C words that are difficult.
D words with their own personality.

3 Which of these statements is NOT true of idioms?

A They sometimes make you laugh.
B They can be puzzling.
C They occur in all languages.
D They spoil the language.

4 Which of these statements is true of idioms?

A They don't make any sense.
B They have no meaning in a sentence.
C They have meanings that can't be understood literally.
D They are words no-one understands.

5 The idiom example *to cost an arm and a leg* is used in the text to show that

A the literal meaning doesn't make sense.
B the literal meaning makes sense.
C people are always making mistakes about word meanings.
D many statements are literally true.

6 Why do idioms cause problems for people learning a new language? Use evidence from the text to explain your answer.

....

....

....

....

Answers and explanations on p. 120

Mixed questions

Use the **Step-by-step guide** on page 4 to help you read the text and answer the questions below. Circle the correct answers or write your answer on the lines.

Huon pine

In the early 19th century, explorers noticed ancient tree trunks buried in the mud of the Huon river, south west of Hobart, Tasmania. They were impressed that the fallen trees had not rotted or suffered from insect damage. They'd come across trunks of the Huon pine, Australia's oldest living tree.

Chained convicts were given the job of cutting down Huon pines and rafting them to Sarah Island, an isolated penal settlement established in Tasmania in 1822. There the logs were sawn and used to build ships for the British Government. Later in the century, piners logged the trees and sold them commercially.

The Huon pine, native only to Tasmania, grows in river bank rainforest in the west and south-west of the island. It reproduces seeds every 5 to 7 years and grows slowly, taking around 1000 years to reach 30 m. The creamy yellow timber contains natural oils, is light, durable and floats when green. These qualities make it much prized for boat building, as well as for making furniture and smaller wooden items.

The scarcity of Huon pine has led to tight control of the industry. 85 per cent of Huon pine forests are now conserved in National Parks, many within the World Heritage Area, and 15 per cent are managed by Forestry Tasmania.

1 What colour is the timber of Huon?

A cream
B creamy yellow
C forest green
D muddy coloured

2 In the words *much prized for boat building*, the word *prized* means

A looked at.
B decorated.
C wondered about.
D highly valued.

3 In the text, *piners* are

A people who cut down Huon pine trees.
B trees that are made of pine.
C people who are lonely because they work in isolated areas.
D people who pine for company.

4 Which occurred first?

A Boats were built on Sarah Island for the British Government.
B Forestry Tasmania took on management of 15 per cent of Huon pine trees.
C Sarah Island was made a penal colony.
D Logging was done commercially in Tasmania.

5 Why is Huon pine chosen as a timber for boat building? Choose all that apply.

A It is much in demand.
B It contains natural oils.
C It can be bought from Forestry Tasmania.
D It is resistant to insects and decay.

6 Why is Huon pine scarce? Use evidence from the text to support your answer.

....

....

....

....

....

....

....

Answers and explanations on pp. 120–121

Mixed questions

Use the **Step-by-step guide** on page 4 to help you read the text and answer the questions below. Circle the correct answers or write your answer on the lines.

To Make Crumbobblious Cutlets

Procure some strips of beef, and, having cut them into the smallest possible slices, proceed to cut them still smaller, eight, or perhaps nine times.

When the whole is thus minced, brush it up hastily with a new clothes-brush, and stir round rapidly and capriciously with a salt-spoon or a soup-ladle.

Place the whole in a saucepan, and remove it to a sunny place—say, the roof of the house, if free from sparrows or other birds—and leave it there for about a week.

At the end of that time add a little lavender, some oil of almonds, and a few herring-bones; and then cover the whole with 4 gallons of clarified Crumbobblious sauce, when it will be ready for use.

Cut it into the shape of ordinary cutlets, and serve up in a clean table-cloth or dinner-napkin.

by Edward Lear, 1870

1. Which word is NOT a synonym for *procure*?
   - **A** eat
   - **B** obtain
   - **C** get
   - **D** find
2. The word *capriciously* means
   - **A** speedily.
   - **B** unpredictably.
   - **C** fast
   - **D** quickly.
3. How does Lear create humour in his recipe? Choose all that apply.
   - **A** through exaggerating
   - **B** by pretending to be serious
   - **C** by including nonsensical ideas
   - **D** by telling jokes
4. What is comical about saying *stir … with a salt-spoon or a soup-ladle*? Choose all that apply.
   - **A** Neither could be used to stir rapidly in this mixture.
   - **B** They are both a type of spoon.
   - **C** They are ridiculously different in size.
   - **D** They are both kitchen utensils.
5. What is comical about *serve up in a clean table-cloth or dinner-napkin*? Choose all that apply.
   - **A** The mixture would fall out.
   - **B** The mixture wouldn't fit.
   - **C** The cloths would need to be laundered.
   - **D** It sounds impolite.
6. Lear doesn't include instructions for the Crumbobblious sauce for the cutlet mixture. Write a short recipe for the sauce in the style of Lear's recipe for cutlets.

Answers and explanations on p. 121

Mixed questions

Use the **Step-by-step guide** on page 4 to help you read the text and answer the questions below. Circle the correct answers or write your answer on the lines.

Seven Little Australians

There was quite a colony of dusty boots in one corner of the room, and there was a great bottle of black, treacly looking varnish on the mantelpiece. Bunty conceived the brilliant idea of cleaning the whole lot and standing them in a neat row to meet his father's delighted eyes. He found a handkerchief on the floor, of superfine cambric, though dirty, poured upon it a liberal allowance of varnish, and attacked the first pair.

A bright polish rewarded him, for they were patent leather ones; but the next and the next and the next would not shine, however hard he rubbed. There was a step on the stair, the firm, well-known step of his father, and he paused a moment with a look of conscious virtue on his small shiny face.

But it fled all at once, and a look of horror replaced it. He had stuck the bottle on a great armchair for convenience, as he was sitting on the floor, and now he noticed it had fallen on its side and a black, horrid stream was issuing from its neck.

And it was the chair with the uniform on, and one of the sleeves was soaked with the stuff, and the beautiful white shirt that lay there, too, waiting for a button, was sticky, horrible! ... The next minute his father was in the room.

From *Seven Little Australians* by Ethel Turner, 1894

1. The word *colony* in the phrase *a colony of dusty boots* means
   - **A** a basketful of objects.
   - **B** a settlement.
   - **C** a group of the same kind of things gathered together.
   - **D** things scattered all over the place.
2. Bunty cleaned the boots because
   - **A** he wanted to please his father.
   - **B** he liked cleaning boots.
   - **C** he liked putting things in rows.
   - **D** he was good at cleaning boots.
3. Which of these events happened last?
   - **A** Bunty put the varnish on the arm of the chair.
   - **B** Bunty took the varnish from the shelf.
   - **C** The varnish spilled on the uniform and the shirt.
   - **D** Barney sat on the floor.
4. When he first heard his father's footsteps, Bunty felt
   - **A** pleased.
   - **B** horrified.
   - **C** virtuous.
   - **D** worried.
5. Bunty is a child who
   - **A** makes a careless mistake.
   - **B** likes to act importantly.
   - **C** is extremely naughty.
   - **D** is dishonest.
6. Predict what you think will happen next in the story.

....

....

....

....

....

Answers and explanations on pp. 121–122

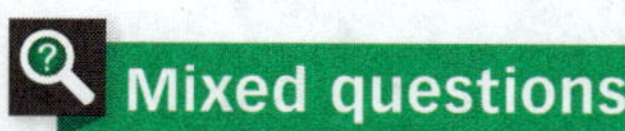

Mixed questions

Use the **Step-by-step guide** on page 4 to help you read the text and answer the questions below. Circle the correct answers or write your answer on the lines.

The Triantiwontigongolope

There's a very funny insect that you do not
often spy,
And it isn't quite a spider, and it isn't quite a fly;
It is something like a beetle, and a little like
a bee,
But nothing like a woolly grub that climbs
upon a tree.
Its name is quite a hard one, but you'll learn
it soon, I hope.
So try:
Tri-
Tri-anti-wonti-
Triantiwontigongolope.

It lives on weeds and wattle-gum, and has a
funny face;
Its appetite is hearty, and its manners a
disgrace.
When first you come upon it, it will give you
quite a scare,
But when you look for it again, you find it
isn't there.
And unless you call it softly it will stay away
and mope.
So try:
Tri-
Tri-anti-wonti-
Triantiwontigongolope.

It trembles if you tickle it or tread upon its toes;
It is not an early riser, but it has a
snubbish nose.
If you sneer at it, or scold it, it will scuttle off
in shame,
But it purrs and purrs quite proudly if you call it
by its name,
And offer it some sandwiches of sealing-wax
and soap.
So try:
Tri-
Tri-anti-wonti-
Triantiwontigongolope.

But of course you haven't seen it; and I
truthfully confess
That I haven't seen it either, and I don't know
its address.
For there isn't such an insect, though there
really might have been
If the trees and grass were purple, and the sky
was bottle green.
It's just a little joke of mine, which you'll forgive,
I hope.
Oh, try!
Tri-
Tri-anti-wonti-
Triantiwontigongolope.

by CJ Dennis, 1821

1 Which of the Triantiwontigongolope's body parts are named in the poem?
- **A** legs, arms, head
- **B** face, toes, nose
- **C** ears, hair, feet
- **D** neck, eyes, elbows

2 What does *sneer* mean?
- **A** smile
- **B** wink
- **C** look scornfully at
- **D** grin

3 The poetic device used to link words together amusingly in the line *It trembles if you tickle it or tread upon its toes* is
- **A** alliteration.
- **B** rhyme.
- **C** rhythm.
- **D** simile.

4 The poet's main purpose is to
- **A** teach the reader how to pronounce the title of his poem.
- **B** teach the reader some science.
- **C** give the reader *quite a scare*.
- **D** amuse the reader with his *little joke*.

5 Where would you find a world where *the trees and grass were purple, and the sky was bottle green*?

....

....

....

....

Answers and explanations on p. 122

ANSWERS

Fact-finding questions

How to throw a frisbee (page 28)

1 A **2** C **3** B **4** C **5** D **6** See below

Explanations

1. This is a **fact-finding** question. **A** is correct. The answer is stated directly in the text. You read *you need … Open space to throw the frisbee* (see lines 2–4). **B** and **C** are incorrect because the text does not include other people or lots of strength in the list of things you need. **D** is the opposite of what is needed as the text states you need to be *clear of trees* (see lines 4–5).
2. This is a **fact-finding** question. **C** is correct. The answer is stated directly in the text. You read in the first instruction that you need to *Stand side on to your target* (see line 7). **A**, **B** and **D** are incorrect because the text does not state you need to stand in those directions.
3. This is a **fact-finding** question. **B** is correct. The answer is stated directly in the text. You read that your index finger should be held *along the edge* (see line 11) of the frisbee. **A** is incorrect because it is the thumb that is placed on the top of the frisbee, not the index finger. **C** and **D** are incorrect because it is your other fingers that are placed in these positions, not your index finger.
4. This is a **fact-finding** question. **C** is correct. The answer is stated directly in the text. You read that your index finger should point *in the direction of your target* (see lines 17–18). In this text the phrase *in the direction of* means the same as *towards*. The positions suggested in **A**, **B** and **D** are different from the instruction the text gives about where your index finger should point; beyond, over and behind do not mean *in the direction of*.
5. This is a **fact-finding** question. **D** is correct. The answer is stated directly in the text. You read in the last sentence that you need to *flick your wrist to release the frisbee* (see line 22). **A**, **B** and **C** describe actions that are used in learning how to throw a frisbee but they are not actions used when releasing the frisbee.
6. This is a **fact-finding** question. The answer is stated directly in the text. The author asks you to *Imagine there is something on the frisbee you don't want to spill* (see lines 19–20) when you are curling your wrist.

Thinking (page 29)

1 C **2** A **3** D **4** B **5** See below

Explanations

1. This is a **fact-finding** question. **C** is correct. The answer is stated directly in the text. The first creature the poet thinks of being is a possum. **A** is incorrect because a tree is not a creature. **B** is incorrect because the poet thinks of being a lizard after she has thought of being a possum. **D** is incorrect because the poet doesn't ever think of being herself—she IS herself!
2. This is a **fact-finding** question. **A** is correct. The answer is stated directly in the text. You read *I'd like to have my own sweet nest. / Yes, I think that might be best* (see lines 8–9). **B** is incorrect because while the poet says it would be fun to be a lizard, she does not say it would be fun to be a bird. **C** and **D** are true statements but the poet does not include these ideas in the poem as reasons for wanting to be a bird.
3. This is a **fact-finding** question. **D** is correct. The answer is stated directly in the text. The poet says that she'd like to be *something that lives in the sea* (see line 11) such as an octopus, whale or fish. **A** and **C** are true of things that live in the sea, but they are not the reasons the poet gives for wanting to be one of those creatures. **B** is incorrect because there is no information about walking long distances in the poem.
4. This is a **fact-finding** question. **B** is correct. The answer is stated directly in the text. The

reason given by the poet for wanting to be a cat is *I'd curl up warm on the fireside mat* (see line 15). **A**, **C** and **D** are things a cat does but the poet doesn't name any of these as reasons for wanting to be a cat.

5 This is a **fact-finding** question. The answer is stated directly in the text. The poet says *In the end I s'pose it's really best / to stay myself and* think *the rest!* (see lines 18–19) This means that she decides it is best to stay as herself and use her imagination to think about being other creatures.

Didgeridoos (page 30)

1 D **2** A **3** D **4** B **5** C **6** See below

Explanations

1 This is a **fact-finding** question. **D** is correct. The answer is stated directly in the text. You read that a *didgeridoo is a musical instrument* (see line 1). **A** is true in that didgeridoos are hollow but this is not what a didgeridoo is. **B** and **C** are also incorrect. Although didgeridoos can be made from a tree branch and they do have paintings decorating them, neither of these things are what a didgeridoo is.

2 This is a **fact-finding** question. **A** is correct. The answer is stated directly in the text. The text states that *Didgeridoos were originally made from tree branches that had been hollowed out by termites* (see lines 7–8). **B** is incorrect. The termites helped hollow out the tree branches but the didgeridoos were not made from termites. **C** is incorrect as the text does not say bamboo was originally used. **D** is incorrect because sticks are what were used to hollow out the tree branches, not to make the didgeridoo itself.

3 This is a **fact-finding** question. **D** is correct. The answer is stated directly in the text. You read that *a stick or hot coals … further clear out the centre* (see lines 9–10). **A** is incorrect because it is only part of what was used. **B** is incorrect because the text states that beeswax and resin were used to make a mouthpiece, not to clear out the didgeridoo. **C** is incorrect because the question asks what was used to further clear out the didgeridoo. The text says that termites help clear out the branches but that they are further cleared out with *a stick or hot coals* (see line 9), not termites.

4 This is a **fact-finding** question. **B** is correct. The answer is stated directly in the text. You read that the player fills his cheeks with air *then blows this into the instrument* [the didgeridoo] (see line 15). **A** and **C** are incorrect because the text does not say the player fills his nose or his throat with air. **D** is incorrect because the text says the musician blows into the instrument, not that he breathes into it.

5 This is a **fact-finding** question. **C** is correct. The answer is stated directly in the text. You read that *This way of breathing and the player's vibrating lips make the pattern of sounds* (see lines 16–18). Both are needed for the sounds to be made. **A** is incorrect because the text does not state that stories of animals and the Dreaming make the pattern of sounds. **B** and **D** only name part of what makes the pattern of sounds.

6 This is a **fact-finding** question. The answer is stated directly in the text. You read that people think didgeridoos are sacred because they are *played at religious ceremonies* (see lines 21–22).

Possums break into bakery (page 31)

1 B **2** A **3** C **4** B **5** See below

Explanations

1 This is a **fact-finding** question. **B** is correct. The answer is stated directly in the text. You read that the possums found their way into the bakery *through a loose board at the back of the kitchen* (see lines 6–7). **A**, **C** and **D** are incorrect because the text does not say that the possums entered through the roof, the wall or the fence.

2 This is a **fact-finding** question. **A** is correct. The answer is stated directly in the text. You read that their home is *next door to the bakery* (see line 13). **B** is incorrect because the lane is behind the bakery and their home, not next door to it. **C** is incorrect because Hobart is a city so their home can't be next door to it. **D** may be true but is incorrect because the text does not tell us anything about their having neighbours.

3 This is a **fact-finding** question. **C** is correct. The answer is stated directly in the text. You read that the sight *gave him* [Mr Flower] *… a big shock* (see lines 17–18). **A** is incorrect because although Mrs Flower may also have got a big shock, this is not stated in the text. **B** and **D** are incorrect because the text does not state how the newspaper reporter or the *Hobart News* reacted to the situation.

4 This is a **fact-finding** question. **B** is correct. The answer is stated directly in the text. You read that *His wife soon discovered another tray with another possum on it. The possum was too full of baked goodies to move so much as a paw* (see lines 21–24). This means that the possum was not moving any part of itself. **A**, **C** and **D** are incorrect as they all say that the possum was moving in some way but it was not moving at all.

5 This is a **fact-finding** question. The answer is stated directly in the text. You read in the last paragraph of the article about what happened in the end to the possums: *Wildlife rescuers caught the possums. They were placed in a box and released back onto the Flowers' roof at nightfall* (see lines 27–29).

Synthesis questions

Our excursion to Chinatown (page 36)

1 C **2** B **3** C **4** B **5** See below

Explanations

1 This is a **synthesis** question. **C** is correct. Tom recounts what happened when Fourth Class went on an excursion to Chinatown. **A** is incorrect because while Chinese culture is described, it is not Tom's purpose in writing the text. **B** is incorrect because the text tells us nothing about Tom's favourite meals. **D** is incorrect because although there is some information about Chinese eating customs, the text is about what happened on the whole excursion, not just at lunchtime.

2 This is a **synthesis** question. **B** is correct. Tom names the arched entrance gate with stone beasts either side as the first thing the class saw when they arrived at Chinatown. The things named in **A**, **C** and **D** are all seen after the students have entered Chinatown. This makes these answers incorrect.

3 This is a **synthesis** question. **C** is correct. There is no mention in the text of using language skills at the Chinese Garden of Friendship. It is described as a *peaceful* (see line 12) place of calm and beauty. **A**, **B** and **D** are incorrect as they include using the Chinese language for various purposes.

4 This is a **synthesis** question. **B** is correct. The student's red face is the only red thing in the list that is not an important part of Chinese culture. **A**, **C** and **D** refer to objects that are red because of the importance of the colour in Chinese culture.

5 This is a **synthesis** question. The last two sentences are written in a more personal way and are mainly about one particular student rather than the excursion itself. For this reason the last two sentences could be cut and the reader would still have a full account of the excursion to Chinatown.

The First Hurdle (page 37)

1 B and D **2** A **3** B **4** A **5** C
6 See below

Explanations

1 This is a **synthesis** question. **B** and **D** are correct. The first time Willa gets goose bumps she has just heard the Killer Plant's high-pitched wail. The second time is after the Killer Plant says how many people it eats daily. **A** is incorrect as the Killer Plant's vanity and foolishness do not make Willa afraid but they help her to think of an escape plan. **C** is incorrect because the Killer Plant does not move slowly.

2 This is a **synthesis** question. **A** is correct. Willa pretends to sound confident to make the Killer Plant think she is unafraid of it. **B** is incorrect because Willa is feeling afraid rather than clever. **C** is incorrect because Willa is not sure she can escape. **D** is incorrect because Willa does not know if the Killer Plant likes confident people.

3 This is a **synthesis** question. **B** is correct. The Killer Plant goes to the lake after Willa has heard him thrashing towards her, noticed his dripping saliva and felt her goose bumps get bigger. **A**, **C** and **D** are incorrect as they all take place before the Killer Plant thrashes towards the lake.

4 This is a **synthesis** question. **A** is correct. When Willa is thinking about the magic spell she is feeling brave and confident, not nervous. **B** and **D** are incorrect because they are signs that Willa is feeling nervous. **C** is incorrect because chewing lazily on the grass stalk is a

way of pretending to be relaxed to hide her nervousness and fear.

5 This is a **synthesis** question. **C** is correct. Willa outwits the Killer Plant with courage and cunning which makes her the heroine of the story. **A** is incorrect because the Rainbow Dragon does nothing in this part of the story. **B** is incorrect because Willa doesn't use the magic spell. **D** is incorrect because being a girl does not make her a heroine.

6 This is a **synthesis** question. The Killer Plant's role in the story is to be the 'baddie' because it is threatening and scary. Its unpleasant behaviour contrasts with Willa's courage and cleverness.

Elizabeth Haywood: a Survivor (page 38)

1 C **2** D **3** A **4** A **5** See below

Explanations

1 This is a **synthesis** question. **C** is correct. The text gives an account of Elizabeth Hayward's life from birth to death. **A**, **B** and **D** are incorrect. They name topics touched on during the account of Elizabeth Hayward's life but they are not the focus of the text as a whole.

2 This is a **synthesis** question. **D** is correct. The events referred to in paragraph one are Elizabeth's birth, her becoming a clogmaker, that she stole from her employer, pawned what she stole and was sentenced to transportation. These events all happened in her early life. **A** is incorrect because in paragraph one we are not given any information about her family, other than that we can assume they were poor. **B** is incorrect as we are not told what Elizabeth enjoyed doing most. **C** is incorrect because paragraph one does not deal with Elizabeth's good behaviour. In fact, it tells us about her stealing.

3 This is a **synthesis** question. **A** is correct. Elizabeth travelled to Botany Bay and to Van Diemen's Land but she had no choice in the matter. **B**, **C** and **D** describe things that actually happened to Elizabeth while she was a convict.

4 This is a **synthesis** question. **A** is correct. We are told that Elizabeth was sent to Norfolk Island two years after she arrived in Sydney, which was in 1790. She is moved from there to Van Diemen's Land in 1813. This means she spent 23 years on Norfolk Island. **B**, **C** and **D** are incorrect as they give the wrong number of years she spent on Norfolk Island.

5 This is a **synthesis** question. Elizabeth's life has many hardships—being put to work at a very young age, living in poverty, being transported as a convict to Australia when young, being whipped and being shipwrecked. She survived all of these trials.

Sculpture by the Sea (page 39)

1 B **2** B **3** D **4** C **5** See below

Explanations

1 This is a **synthesis** question. **B** is correct. The main purpose of the text is to give information about the Sydney event, Sculpture by the Sea. It describes what it is, its history and its successes. **A** is incorrect as there are no instructions given about how to create a sculpture in the text. **C** is incorrect as directions to the event are not included. **D** is incorrect because while sculptors may be encouraged to show their work by learning about the huge audiences that attend, this is not the text's main purpose.

2 This is a **synthesis** question. **B** is correct. You read *The idea was sparked by his* [Handley's] *visit to an outdoor sculpture park … in Bohemia* (see lines 8–9). It was this visit which led to the first Sculpture by the Sea exhibition in Sydney in 1997. This event happened before the first Danish event and the 2014 Sydney event. **A**, **C** and **D** are incorrect because they all happened after Handley's visit to Bohemia which took place some time before 1997: **A** in 1997, **C** in 2009 and **D** in 2014.

3 This is a **synthesis** question. **D** is correct. There is no information given about what sculptors need to do to have their work accepted for the Sculpture by the Sea exhibition. **A** is incorrect because the text includes information about David Handley, the person who *dreamed up* (see line 7) the event. **B** is incorrect because the text says up to *half a million people walk the coastal track each year* (see line 14). **C** is incorrect because we are told the cost is nothing as the event is *free* (see line 7).

4 This is a **synthesis** question. **C** is correct. In order to visit Sculpture by the Sea, tourists would need to know when it is open and how to get there. **A**, **B** and **D** are incorrect because information about the prizes offered, Princess

Mary's visit or the Bohemian ruins would not be of any use to tourists wanting to make a visit.

5 This is a **synthesis** question. If you compare the information given about each event it is clear that both are free, both are held annually and both use the coastline to display sculptures along a walk.

Inferring questions

My trip to South America (page 44)

1 C **2** C **3** B **4** A **5** See below

Explanations

1 This is an **inferring** question. **C** is correct. Brazil and Peru are place names that refer to countries that Theo has visited. The map confirms that they are countries rather than cities. **A** is incorrect because Ipanema is named as a beach in the text and it is implied that Rio de Janeiro is a city in Brazil. Neither of these places are included as the names of countries on the map. **B** is incorrect because it is implied that Rio de Janeiro is a city in Brazil. **D** is incorrect because Chile is described in the text as a place Theo hasn't yet visited.

2 This is an **inferring** question. **C** is correct. The text says Theo *sang that* (e.g. 'The Girl from Ipanema') *(see line 7)*, which means it is a song about a girl. **A**, **B** and **D** are incorrect because none are songs so they can't be sung.

3 This is an **inferring** question. **B** is correct. It is implied that the high passes they hike along are part of the Andes. High passes are normally found in the mountains. **A** is incorrect because you can't hike through a race of people. **C** is incorrect because the Inca Trail is a walking track itself. **D** is incorrect because you can't hike through lakes.

4 This is an **inferring** question. **A** is correct. We are told that Machu Picchu was built in 1450, which is hundreds of years ago. **B** is incorrect because the Incas were living hundreds of years ago. **C** and **D** are incorrect because people living at the time of Theo's visit were not alive when the Incas were living in Machu Picchu.

5 This is an **inferring** question. You can work out that:
- since the Incas didn't return to Peru after the Spanish conquest, it is likely that the Spanish kept control of it.
- since Theo practises his Spanish with Spanish-speaking people when he is in Peru, Spanish is still spoken there. This suggests that the Spanish conquest was successful as they still occupy the area.

Life cycle of the frog (page 45)

1 A and C **2** C **3** A **4** B **5** See below

Explanations

1 This is an **inferring** question. **A** and **C** are correct. The text says the eggs are *left floating in the water* (see line 3). This implies they are not protected by their parents. It also means they can be eaten by other animals. **B** is incorrect as water is the environment in which frogs' eggs grow and develop. It does not cause them to drown. **D** is incorrect as the jelly is added to cover the eggs and becomes a source of food. The eggs do not turn into jelly.

2 This is an **inferring** question. **C** is correct. The pattern is that each cell splits into two more cells. If there are eight cells then it is implied that the next number will be 16 cells, or eight times two. **A**, **B** and **D** are incorrect as they don't follow the pattern of development that is described.

3 This is an **inferring** question. **A** is correct. The tadpole develops legs late in the cycle. This implies that they are needed for the next stage of its development. The tadpole grows legs to use for hopping on land as an adult frog. **B**, **C** and **D** are incorrect because they assume that legs help the tadpole swim more quickly in the water. The tadpole uses its tail to help it do these things, not its legs.

4 This is an **inferring** question. **B** is correct. Tadpoles have gills for breathing under water but these are replaced by lungs as they turn into frogs, which live mostly on land. They need lungs to breathe air to stay alive. **A** and **D** are incorrect because lungs can't be used for breathing in the water. **C** is incorrect because lungs are inside the frog's body and so can't be used to catch insects.

5 This is an **inferring** question. You can infer that the tadpole's body is smaller than that of an adult frog. Tadpoles have gills for breathing

and a tail for swimming. Frogs have legs for hopping and lungs for breathing.

The Second Hurdle (page 46)

1 C **2** B **3** D **4** C **5** See below

Explanations

1. This is an **inferring** question. **C** is correct. We are told that when Willa stepped from the darkness of the forest into the light, her eyes were dazzled. This implies that it was hard for her to see what was in front of her and is what caused her to nearly fall into the chasm. **A** and **B** are accurate descriptions of the chasm but they do not explain why Willa nearly fell, which makes them incorrect. **D** is incorrect because Willa only became unsteady after the light had dazzled her eyes.
2. This is an **inferring** question. **B** is correct. Willa sees that she can't cross the chasm because it appears to be *bottomless* and *wider than the sun* (see lines 5–6). This means you would have to fly across the chasm to get to the other side. The pterosaur is able to do that. **A** is incorrect because although the pterosaur is powerful, this is only part of the reason that he can cross the chasm when Willa can't. **C** is incorrect because even though the pterosaur may have magic powers, it is his being able to fly that will get him across that very wide space. **D** is incorrect because there is no mention of the pterosaur knowing about a secret path. He plans to fly Willa over the chasm.
3. This is an **inferring** question. **D** is correct. The information Willa had about the pterosaur came from reading an article in the newspaper. You can infer that this must be where Willa learned that it lived in the age of the dinosaurs. **A** is incorrect because looking old implies you were born a long time ago, but not necessarily as long ago as in the age of the dinosaurs. **B** is incorrect because Willa not having seen a live pterosaur before doesn't prove anything about when pterosaurs lived. **C** is incorrect because a croaky voice is not a sign of living in the age of dinosaurs.
4. This is an **inferring** question. **C** is correct. At first the pterosaur's voice is croaky but when he names the witch his voice trembles. This is a strong hint that he is afraid of her. It suggests he has had trouble with the witch in the past. **A** is incorrect as the pterosaur and his wife have eaten the witch's berries before. **B** is incorrect. It is true that the word *witch* usually names someone who is scary but it is because the pterosaur has met the witch before and knows she is scary that his voice trembles. **D** may or may not be true but it is not information given in the story so it is an incorrect answer.
5. This is an **inferring** question. Willa had believed that witches were only found in story books. Now that the pterosaur sounds scared of the person he calls the Wicked Witch of the Ditch, she has doubts she was right. She thinks for a moment that maybe there are witches in real life!

Should you feed wild birds? (1) (page 47)

1 B **2** A **3** A **4** B **5** D **6** See below

Explanations

1. This is an **inferring** question. **B** is correct. The natural toxin referred to in the text comes from the salted or roasted peanuts. This implies that it comes from the peanuts themselves and is not an added substance. It is harmful to birds as eating it can poison them. **A** and **C** are incorrect as there is no evidence in the text to suggest what a natural toxin tastes like. **D** is incorrect because this is not stated in the text.
2. This is an **inferring** question. **A** is correct. You read that damaged feathers *can affect waterproofing as well as a bird's ability to maintain body temperature and even to fly* (see lines 6–7). You can infer that these are serious consequences because they are life threatening. **B** and **C** are incorrect because they are untrue but also because they are about how birds appear to humans. This has nothing to do with why the damaged feathers are a problem for birds. **D** is incorrect because there is no evidence in the text that damaged feathers can be mended.
3. This is an **inferring** question. **A** is correct. The sentence implies that the risk you take when you feed wild birds is you may harm them and it is not worth taking this risk. **B** is incorrect because the sentence implies you should not take risks which is the opposite of what the sentence means. **C** is incorrect because although the sentence implies you shouldn't take risks by feeding birds, it does not imply

people should never take risks. **D** is incorrect because it is the opposite of what Marissa is arguing. She is suggesting it is never worth taking the risk of feeding wild birds as it could be harmful.

4 This is an **inferring** question. **B** is correct. You can infer that natural food for birds in this sentence refers to food they can find for themselves, such as berries and seeds from plants and trees. **A** and **C** are incorrect because these are foods sold in shops rather than being found in nature on plants and trees. **D** is incorrect because food left out by humans is what birds eat when it is available to them. It is the opposite of the kind of food referred to in the sentence.

5 This is an **inferring** question. **D** is correct. The only people who can keep the feeders clean are those who put out the feed for the birds. You can infer that these people are responsible for spreading disease if they don't keep the feeders clean. **A** and **C** are incorrect as birds can't be held responsible for keeping feeders clean. **B** is incorrect because while some of those who believe in feeding wild birds may not have kept feeders clean and so caused birds to die of disease, not all of these people would fail to keep feeders clean.

6 This is an **inferring** question. Marissa thinks birds are more likely to stay alive if they get their food from nature. By saying she prefers her birds alive she is confirming her view that people should NOT feed wild birds as they are likely to end up harmed or dead.

My childhood memories (page 48)

1 B, C and D **2** C **3** A and D **4** B **5** B
6 See below

Explanations

1 This is an **inferring** question. **B**, **C** and **D** are correct. You can work out that ice would be put into an icebox to stop it melting and that the ice would then be used for cooling drinks and keeping food cool so it didn't go bad. **A** is incorrect because you would not need ice delivered if you lived near the North Pole.

2 This is an **inferring** question. **C** is correct. The text says *It* [the tooth] *had come out by itself!* *(see line 8)* This implies the hard thing bitten on in the sandwich was the tooth. **A**, **B** and **D** are incorrect. They are not referred to in the text and they are not the tooth.

3 This is an **inferring** question. **A** and **D** are correct. The presents are hidden and Sam should not be looking at them. Feelings of guilt about doing the wrong thing and fear of being caught are the reasons Sam hides in the wardrobe. **B** is incorrect as Sam is not trying to hear better but to hide. **C** is incorrect as there is no evidence in the text that Sam wants to scare anyone.

4 This is an **inferring** question. **B** is correct. The memories are from Sam's childhood. The appliances from Sam's home were common around 60 years ago and are not from a modern household. This implies that Sam is 50 or more. **A** is incorrect because Sam's memories are from many years ago. **C** and **D** are incorrect as there is no evidence as to whether Sam is male or female. The name, Sam, is commonly used for both sexes.

5 This is an **inferring** question. **B** is correct. Sam had begged to take the pup home and already loved it so would have been very disappointed not to be allowed to keep it. **A**, **C** and **D** are incorrect as they are feelings that are the opposite of those it is implied Sam would have felt.

6 This is an **inferring** question. Sam's family had an icebox and a turntable record player. This means Sam probably grew up without a fridge or a CD player. As Sam had to lie on the floor to keep cool it seems likely that the family did not have an air conditioner either.

Should children have to earn their pocket money? (page 49)

1 B **2** B **3** A **4** B **5** D **6** See below

Explanations

1 This is an **inferring** question. **B** is correct. Chilli agrees with her parents about not earning pocket money but she disagrees with their not letting her do extra tasks for extra money. **A** is incorrect because it is the opposite of what her parents think and she agrees with them. **C** is incorrect because she thinks it is good for extra pocket money to be earned for doing extra things around the house. **D** is incorrect because neither her parents nor Chilli agree with this view.

2 This is an **inferring** question. **B** is correct. Connie says her family believes you should do chores to earn pocket money and not be paid if you fail to do them and she completely agrees with their view. **A** is incorrect as Chilli thinks you should be allowed to do extra tasks for money and her parents don't agree. **C** and **D** are incorrect as neither Ricardo nor Alice tells us what their parents' views are. This means we don't know if they agree with their parents or not.

3 This is an **inferring** question. **A** is correct. You can infer that Celine is in the role of a compere on the programme and not one of the students taking part. Nothing Celine says expresses her point of view on the topic. Her role is to ask the children to share their points of view. This makes **B**, **C** and **D** incorrect as they assume Celine expresses an opinion of her own.

4 This is an **inferring** question. **B** is correct. You can infer that Ricardo agrees with Connie who strongly approves of the idea of being paid pocket money for doing chores. Ricardo adds another point in its favour—that it teaches you the skills you need to manage money. **A** is incorrect because it is the opposite of what he says. **C** is incorrect as it implies he approves of the no strings idea which is untrue. **D** is incorrect because he agrees with Connie who is strongly opposed to the idea of pocket money with no strings.

5 This is an **inferring** question. **D** is correct. You can infer that Alice thinks children should not be paid for helping in the home. In her view linking helping in the home with earning teaches children the wrong values. **A** is incorrect as it is the opposite of the opinion she gives. **B** is incorrect because she strongly supports the idea and does not express any doubts about it. **C** is incorrect because she expresses strong approval for the idea.

6 This is an **inferring** question. When Celine asks if children think *pocket money with no strings is a good idea* (see line 12) you can infer that she is asking if others agree with what Chilli has just said about her parents' views on pocket money. In other words pocket money with no strings means that pocket money should be given freely and not tied to doing chores.

Jim Jones at Botany Bay (page 50)

1 C **2** D **3** A **4** D **5** See below

Explanations

1 This is an **inferring** question. **C** is correct. You can infer that Jim Jones dreads going to Botany Bay because he thinks his life as a convict there will be unbearable. Living the life of a pirate with all its dangers seems a better idea to him. **A** and **D** may or may not be true but neither gives the reason implied in the text for his saying he'd rather be on the pirate ship. This makes them incorrect. **B** is not the reason given for wanting to be off his ship so it is also incorrect.

2 This is an **inferring** question. **D** is correct. You can infer that Jim Jones thinks that being flogged and toiling his life away in chains is a worse prospect than losing his life by drowning in a terrible storm. **A** is incorrect because there is no mention of Jim Jones being made seasick and it is not a reason for him to prefer drowning to living the life of a convict. **B** is incorrect because the storms making Jim Jones miserable are not the reason he'd prefer to drown than travel to NSW. **C** is incorrect because this is the opposite of what he thinks. He thinks he should be set free.

3 This is an **inferring** question. **A** is correct. Jim is a convict being transported to Botany Bay. He says he plans to *slip* (see line 12) from his chains to escape some day. This implies that convicts are put in chains to prevent them from escaping. **B** is incorrect because Jim dreams that being a bushranger will bring him freedom from chains. **C** is incorrect because Jim is referring to the iron chains around his legs that prevent him escaping, not to blocks of iron or carrying these on his back. **D** is incorrect because he won't be buying the iron and it isn't clothing. The iron he will wear will be around his limbs to keep him from escaping.

4 This is an **inferring** question. **D** is correct. You can infer that Jim Jones thinks the bushrangers are brave because he admires their ability to stay free from the authority and control of others. **A** and **B** are incorrect because Jim could not have met Jack Donahue or other bushrangers as he is still on the ship bringing him to Australia. What Jim knows

about bushrangers he has learned from what *they say* (see line 8), or what other people have told him. **C** may be partly true as Jim does want to be a bushranger but it is not the whole reason as he compliments them on their strength in keeping free of authority.

5 This is an **inferring** question. You can infer that Jim despises and hates the floggers who punish convicts and wants to get his revenge on them. His plan to *gun the floggers down* (see line 15) implies he would like to kill them for how he thinks they will treat him in Botany Bay.

Alice in Wonderland (page 51)

1 D **2** A **3** B **4** A **5** See below

Explanations

1 This is an **inferring** question. **D** is correct. When Alice considers making a daisy chain, you can infer that she is comparing the pleasure she would get with the effort she would have to make to get that pleasure. This keeps her from getting started. **A** is incorrect as it is only part of what is stopping her. **B** is incorrect as the opposite is true—Alice likes daisies enough to think making a daisy chain would be pleasurable. **C** is incorrect as it is implied in the text that Alice sees some daisies she could pick for her daisy chain.

2 This is an **inferring** question. **A** is correct. That the White Rabbit talked could have amazed Alice but she hardly noticed at the time. You can infer it was its taking a watch from its waistcoat pocket that amazed her. **B** and **C** are incorrect as they are things that a normal rabbit might do or look like. **D** is incorrect as the White Rabbit doesn't stop to look at Alice but races past her.

3 This is an **inferring** question. **B** is correct. You can infer that the White Rabbit was not frightened by Alice. He hurried past her because he was anxious about being late and didn't really notice her at the time. **A** and **C** are incorrect as there is no information about Alice's size or how she sat in this text. Neither is relevant as the rabbit rushes past without taking notice of her. **D** is incorrect. Rabbits are usually afraid of humans which makes it a likely reason for running past quickly, but as this rabbit is unusual we can't assume it is or isn't afraid of Alice.

4 This is an **inferring** question. **A** is correct. Alice's curiosity grows very strong when she realises she has just seen a White Rabbit who is dressed in a waistcoat and has his very own pocket watch. She wants to find out more about this unusual rabbit before it disappears. **B** is incorrect as Alice's curiosity isn't burning her in the sense of making her hot and bothered. **C** is incorrect because there is no cat in this story as yet! (You may know that 'curiosity killed the cat' is an idiom meaning being too inquisitive can get you into trouble, which could be true for Alice, but it is not being used like that in this question.) **D** is partly true as Alice may wish to talk to the White Rabbit but this is only one thing she might want to do. She might also want to watch where it is going, see where it lives or find out what it is late for.

5 This is an **inferring** question. If you don't know the story you can predict that, as this is a narrative, what happens next will move the story forward. It seems likely that Alice will follow the rabbit since so much time has been spent describing how it interests her. You can infer that Alice will probably continue down the rabbit-hole especially as you read that she went down it *never once considering how in the world she was to get out again* (see lines 20–22). The title *Alice in Wonderland* also gives readers the clue that she ends up somewhere different from the real world. Maybe she is on her way to a Wonderland where White Rabbits wear waistcoats and can tell the time! If you know the story of *Alice in Wonderland* you will know that these predictions are close to what really happens!

Language questions

Kwanza the white lion (page 56)

1 B **2** A **3** B **4** A **5** C **6** See below

Explanations

1 This is a **language** question. **B** is correct. The words *soft and cuddly* (see line 6) mean the white lion looks as if he would be nice to cuddle. The words 'to me' are not included in Benji's sentence but they are understood: *Kwanza looks soft and cuddly* (to me). **A** is incorrect. A scientist might use the word *soft* to describe a white lion's fur but the word *cuddly* is not a

scientific term. It describes how Kwanza looks to Benji. **C** is incorrect. These words might remind the reader of a laundry commercial but they are not there for that purpose. **D** is incorrect as it is Benji's voice talking to his Diary that we hear, not the zoo owner's voice. The zoo owner doesn't say how Kwanza looks to her in the text.

2 This is a **language** question. **A** is correct. The zoo owner is talking about herself being still loved by Kwanza. The inverted commas around the word '*mum*' are used to show that the zoo owner is not his real mother but that she is in the role of a mother to him. She says he shows this by often trying *to sit in her lap and suck her finger* (see lines 9–10). **B** is incorrect as inverted commas are not being used to indicate the zoo owner's importance. **C** is incorrect because Kwanza's real mum is a lion, not a person. **D** is incorrect because the zoo owner is talking about herself, not someone she hasn't met.

3 This is a **language** question. **B** is correct. Benji thinks it surprising that a lion and a dog like exploring and playing together but *even* (see line 13) more surprising for a lion and a dog to play at wrestling. **A** may be true but the word *even* expresses his surprise rather than his anxiety. **C** is incorrect as *also* means 'in addition' or 'as well', which is not what it means in this context. **D** is incorrect because the opposite is true. Benji sees them wrestle playfully together.

4 This is a **language** question. **A** is correct. Benji includes the word *you* as a way of talking to his audience (his diary) in a personal, friendly way. **B**, **C** and **D** are incorrect as they mean the opposite of friendly.

5 This is a **language** question. **C** is correct. Parts of the words *fantastic* and *fabulous* are blended together to make the word *fantabulous* (see line 19). It is a way of expressing the idea that Benji thought his visit to see the white lion was extra special. **A** is incorrect because *fantabulous* is an English word made from two other English words. **B** is incorrect because *fantabulous* does have meaning in this context. **D** is incorrect because *fantabulous* is not a word that you would use in very formal writing. It suits a diary, which is informal and personal.

6 This is a **language** question. When Benji writes to his diary he talks to it as though it were a real person. He writes as if it listens to him and wants to hear about his thoughts, feelings and activities. He treats it as an interested and sympathetic friend.

Corroboree, Sydney (page 57)

1 C **2** A **3** C **4** B **5** A **6** See below

Explanations

1 This is a **language** question. **C** is correct. The word *catch* in the sentence *You can catch her at Corroboree, Sydney* (see line 4) is a casual way of saying you can see Casey Donovan singing. **A**, **B**, and **D** are incorrect. None of these words add a casual, relaxed tone to its sentence as each is used quite formally.

2 This is a **language** question. **A** is correct. The word *documented* (see line 7) means evidence that is recorded for others to know about. In this case it was probably a written record. **B** and **D** are incorrect. Hearing or viewing the corroboree is not the same as documenting it though both may have been part of the process. **C** is incorrect as the explorers watched the corroboree being performed; they did not perform it themselves.

3 This is a **language** question. **C** is correct. To describe the events as *stunning* (see line 11) is to give them a very high approval rating. It suggests that if you don't see them you will be missing out on something important and wonderful. **A** and **B** are incorrect because the words *first* and *early* (see lines 6–7) are linked with things from the past that you won't see at Corroboree, Sydney. **D** is incorrect as the word *Royal* is part of a place name. It is not being used to persuade the listener to attend Corroboree, Sydney.

4 This is a **language** question. **B** is correct. Bennelong is a person who belonged to the *Wangal people* (see lines 12–13). Bennelong Point has been named after him. **A**, **C** and **D** are all names of First Australian peoples referred to in the text.

5 This is a **language** question. **A** is correct. The expression *think again* (see line 17) is a saying or idiom that means 'you are wrong'. The announcer says this not to make the listeners feel they are in the wrong but to emphasise that there are events for children and to bring them along as well. **B** and **C** are incorrect because although the saying *think again* means 'you are wrong', the announcer's purpose is to remind listeners of something, not to make them feel bad about themselves. **D** is incorrect because the announcer wants to encourage children to attend as well as adults.

6 This is a **language** question. The announcer would sound encouraging and confident about the advice to visit events at *Corroboree, Sydney*. They are offered in the form of a friendly command that you should attend an event at *Corroboree, Sydney* or you'll miss out on a wonderful experience.

Ming the Mollusc (page 58)

1 B **2** C **3** B and C **4** C **5** See below

Explanations

1 This is a **language** question. **B** is correct. It is Ming, the mollusc of the title, whose voice narrates the poem. You read *I am a mollusc old and rare* (see line 7) and the narrator refers to itself as *me* and *I* throughout the poem. **A**, **C** and **D** are incorrect as none of these have a voice of the poem.

2 This is a **language** question. **C** is correct. The poem is an account of a scientific mistake (a wrong counting) told in a lighthearted way from the perspective of the mollusc. It aims to amuse and entertain the reader. **A** is incorrect as the poem is not about climate change. **B** is incorrect because although the poem refers to a counting error, that is only part of what the poem is about and not its main purpose. **C** is incorrect. The poem recognises that the scientists who counted the layers on Ming's shell made a mistake but it does not suggest scientists as a group are dangerous people.

3 This is a **language** question. **B** and **C** are correct. The expression Ming uses would normally be *I've seen a thing or two* (see line 20). By doubling two to four, Ming is joking that it has lived so long it has seen twice as much as everyone else. Ming also needed to make *four* rhyme with *more* to keep the rhyming pattern of the poem. **A** is incorrect as Ming says *four* instead of *two* deliberately to make a joke. **D** is incorrect as there is no evidence as to how many eyes Ming has. This is not its reason for using the expression.

4 This is a **language** question. **C** is correct. You would not expect to find a poem in a scientific textbook. The poem is about a scientific subject but it is treated in a humorous, not a scientific, way. **A**, **B** and **D** are all publications which could include a poem of this kind.

5 This is a **language** question. Ming uses language through the poem that draws attention to the mistakes the scientists have made in their research (e.g. *counted wrong*; *looked again and found / now* (see lines 13 and 15–16)). This suggests Ming is very doubtful about the scientists' abilities to learn from their research. At the end of the poem, however, Ming says: *Have I helped them learn new things? Truth is I'm not certain.* This suggests he can't really decide whether or not the research has been useful. He also doesn't care much about it any more now he is a ghost.

Night Noodle Markets (page 59)

1 C **2** B **3** A **4** C **5** A **6** See below

Explanations

1 This is a **language** question. **C** is correct. The letters in *niftynoodlesatnight.com.au* (see line 2) make up the address of the website. Clicking on this combination of letters would usually take you to the website. **A** is incorrect because the letters are not arranged in the form of a person's name. **B** is incorrect because the letters do have meaning as an address for a website. **D** is incorrect because the letters are not the name of the markets. If you separate the words (*nifty noodles at night*) they give the viewer some information about what the website is about, but their name is Night Noodle Markets which is different.

2 This is a **language** question. **B** is correct. Words such as *awesome*, *delicious* and *tantalise* (see lines 3 and 5) and the images of delicious food aim to entice viewers to the markets. **A** is incorrect because the type of language and images used are not aiming to be unusual. They are chosen to persuade the viewer that they want to see and taste what is on offer at the markets. **C** is incorrect because the language and the images aim to be the opposite of off-putting. **D** is incorrect because informal language such as *lap up* and *take a peek* (see lines 6 and 8) is included.

3 This is a **language** question. **A** is correct. The word *Fragrant* when it is describing food means aromas that smell attractive. Things that smell attractive appeal to the sense of smell. **B**, **C** and **D** are incorrect. Hearing, touch and sight are not the senses used to smell things.

4 This is a **language** question. **B** is correct. The idiom *kick off* (see line 10), taken from football, means 'begin' or 'get started' in this context. It tells the viewer that the Night Noodle Markets open to the public at 5 pm. **A**, **C** and **D** are incorrect because they mean the opposite of begin.

5 This is a **language** question. **A** is correct. The word *cuisine* (see line 8) refers to a style of cooking typical of a particular region or area. In this case Chinese, Japanese, Indian, Malaysian, Thai, Vietnamese and Singaporean cuisines are mentioned. **B**, **C** and **D** are incorrect because they name particular foods or types of food and not styles of cooking.

6 This is a **language** question. The words *Click on* and *Download* (see lines 8 and 12) are instructions that people using websites follow when they want to find out more information. Readers of newspapers won't be successful if they follow these instructions. Clicking on a newspaper won't bring up more information and you can't download information by touching a newspaper (unless it has been coded in a way that allows you to use technology to do so).

George Raper: a short life (page 60)

1 B **2** D **3** D **4** A **5** A **6** See below

Explanations

1 This is a **language** question. **B** is correct. The word *short* in the title suggests George Raper did not have a long life. He died at the age of 27, which is a young age to die. **A** is incorrect because *short* does not mean the opposite of tall in this context. **C** is incorrect because the word *short* describes George Raper's life, not the text itself. **D** is incorrect because although *short* can mean 'to go without', this meaning does not make sense in the title.

2 This is a **language** question. **D** is correct. The text records details of George Raper's life and reputation in the formal language of a biography. **A** is incorrect as the language is not technical or scientific. **B** is incorrect as the details of Raper's life are described without eye-catching headlines or colourful language. **C** is incorrect as the language is not as personal as that used in letters to family or friends.

3 This is a **language** question. **D** is correct. The context makes it clear that an *able seaman* (see line 6) is a rank in the navy. It is a higher rank than that of a captain's servant and lower than that of a lieutenant. **A** is incorrect. An *able seaman* is a rank, not a person. **B** is incorrect as an *able seaman* is a lower rank than that of lieutenant. **C** is incorrect as while an *able seaman* may be a fit young man, this is not what defines the term. It describes a rank in the navy.

4 This is a **language** question. **A** is correct. The *documents* (see line 19) are accurate records of how the natural world and its plants and animals looked at the time. They provide information about Australia's history. **B** is incorrect as the word *documents* in this context refers to maps and paintings, not to handwritten accounts. **C** is incorrect because the maps and paintings are more than ideas. They are illustrations of the natural world and its plants and animals in the late 18th century. **D** is incorrect because men's and women's stories are not included in the named documents.

5 This is a **language** question. **A** is correct. You read *He gained a place on the* Sirius *bound for Botany Bay* (see lines 6–7). The *Sirius* was going to Botany Bay, Australia, when it left England. **B**, **C** and **D** are incorrect because these senses of *bound* do not fit in this context.

6 This is a **language** question. In this context, the term *footnote* (see line 21) means something added as a new piece of information at the end or foot of the text. It tells about something relevant to Raper's life story that has only recently been discovered.

The Third Hurdle (page 61)

1 B **2** C **3** A **4** A **5** B **6** See below

Explanations

1 This is a **language** question. **B** is correct. The text says the Guard *trumpeted* the words *RD's Guard here* (see line 6) when he first appears. This means his voice booms out loudly like

a trumpet and he uses his title (Rainbow Dragon's Guard), not his name, to announce himself. **A** is incorrect as his words are trumpeted, which is the opposite of whispering. **C** is incorrect as there is no mention of him either giggling or snorting (though it is easy to imagine him doing both of these things!) **D** is incorrect as it is not suggested he *trumpeted* in a singsong way.

2 This is a **language** question. **C** is correct. In order to get inside the stone door Willa has to get past the guard. She uses the words *most important* (see line 9) to flatter him so she can trick him into doing what she wants. **A** is incorrect as there is only one guard and Willa is only pretending to think he is important. **B** is true as Willa is pretending to be friendly but to get him to listen to her she needs to go further by flattering him. **D** is true but it is not the reason she refers to him as the Dragon's *most important* guard.

3 This is a **language** question. **A** is correct. The guard is delighted to hear himself described as important and shows this by *smugly* (see line 10) agreeing with that description of himself, even though he seems to be the only guard. This shows the reader that he is full of vanity. **B** is incorrect as the word *ugly* is different from *smugly* and it describes appearance not character. **C** and **D** are incorrect as there is no evidence that the guard acts in either of these ways.

4 This is a **language** question. **A** is correct. He starts to say this by mistake. It shows he wants the gift for himself but doesn't mean to tell Willa that. He pretends he is talking about the kind of gift the Rainbow Dragon accepts. **B** may be true but it is not the reason he first says *I* instead of *he* (see line 12). **C** is incorrect because there is no evidence that he has trouble with his words. **D** is incorrect as his mistake is a slip of the tongue which he does not mean to make.

5 This is a **language** question. **B** is correct. The word *whe e e e e w* is spelt the way it sounds. The spaces draw out the middle sound to lengthen the word so it sounds as if Willa is letting out her breath and sighing with relief. **A** is incorrect because *whe e e e e w* is one word that is spelt in an unusual way, not seven separate words. **C** is incorrect because *whe e e e e w* is an exclamation of relief, not an example of stuttering. **D** is incorrect because the spaces in the word *whe e e e e w* are put there deliberately by the author to create the sound Willa makes as she expresses her relief.

6 This is a **language** question. The idiom *done and dusted* (see line 21) means that Willa feels she has successfully completed her mission. She has prevented the Guard from stopping her entry into the Rainbow Dragon's home and is over the third hurdle that has stood in her way.

Words under the microscope (page 62)

1 B **2** A **3** A **4** D **5** See below

Explanations

1 This is a **language** question. **B** is correct. The idiom *under the microscope* means to look at something very closely to find out more about it. It doesn't refer to an actual microscope but to its function of making things clearer. **A** is incorrect because a computer screen has nothing to do with the idea expressed by the idiom. **C** is incorrect because the idiom is not to be understood literally. It does not mean words are put under a real microscope. **D** is incorrect because enlarging is what an actual microscope does. The idiom suggests words are to be looked at closely, not literally made bigger or enlarged.

2 This is a **language** question. **A** is correct. The word *Take* (see line 7) in this text is used to invite the reader to think about the word *Tuesday* in a friendly, relaxed way. **B** is incorrect as *Take* Tuesday is an informal way of speaking, the opposite of uptight and formal. **C** is incorrect as the words are not impolite or rude, just relaxed. **D** is incorrect as *Take* Tuesday is a grammatically correct sentence. Its subject *you* is understood and it has a verb and an object. It also has a meaning which makes sense.

3 This is a **language** question. **A** is correct. You can't hold footsteps as they are ever moving; you can't hold a woman's beard as it doesn't exist; you can't hold the breath of a fish as it evaporates. **B** is incorrect because the things named are not objects and there is no way you could hold them. **C** is incorrect because although they are invisible to the human eye they are not imaginary and they are not objects. **D** is incorrect because they are not items and they can't be put in a shopping trolley.

4 This is a **language** question. **D** is correct. *Blend* means to combine parts together so they become one thing. The examples of *blended* (see line 22) words given in the text combine parts of words. **A** and **B** are incorrect because whole words are not used to make blended words. **C** is incorrect because letters stay in their correct order and are added together rather than mixed up.

5 This is a **language** question. The words *emailing, blogging* and *googling* (see line 24) are activities that didn't exist in the time of our great-great-grandparents so would have sounded like meaningless nonsense to them. They are words that came into the language in the late 20th century, well after the invention of the internet.

The seahorse (page 63)

1 D **2** A **3** D **4** C **5** A **6** See below

Explanations

1 This is a **language** question. **D** is correct. The seahorse recounts reasons for feeling sorrowful and hopes to cheer up. You can work out from this context that the seahorse's lament is an expression of sorrow, or a sad tale. **A, B** and **C** are incorrect as the text is not a poem, conversation or debate. For this reason words with these meanings would not be used in the title.

2 This is a **language** question. **A** is correct. The seahorse's lament is told in the first person (*I*) from the seahorse's point of view. This makes **B** and **C** incorrect as the second person (*you*) and the third person (*he, she, it* or *they*) are not used to voice the lament. **D** is incorrect because the text is told in the voice of the seahorse using the first person.

3 This is a **language** question. **D** is correct. The word *Maybe* (see line 6) is the only modal word used in the text that suggests any doubt. **A** and **B** are used to express certainty. The word *so* in **C** is used in the sense of 'very' and also expresses certainty.

4 This is a **language** question. **C** is correct. The author uses the third-person pronouns *it* and *they* to report information about the seahorse's unusual features. This makes **A** and **B** incorrect as the first person (*I, we*) and the second person (*you*) are not used. **D** is incorrect because the text is told in the voice of the author reporting the information.

5 This is a **language** question. **A** is correct. The wording of Text 2 is informative as it gives information about the unusual features of the seahorse. **B** is incorrect because the writer is not making up or creating this information but reporting facts which make the seahorse unusual. **C** is incorrect because the author is not reflecting on seahorses but reporting about them. **D** is incorrect because the author is not using persuasive language to convince you of a point of view.

6 This is a **language** question. Labels could include:

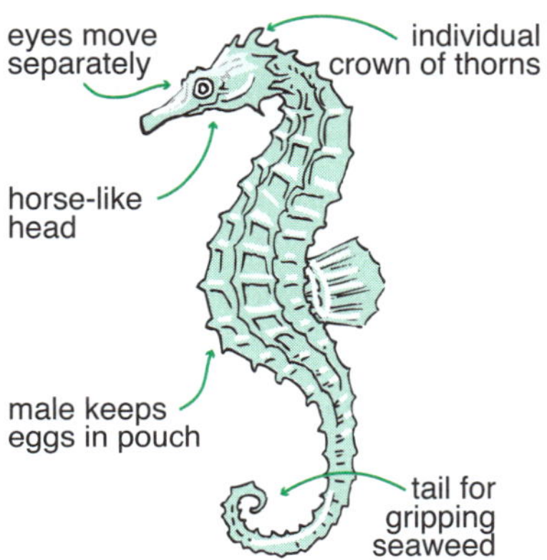

Judgement questions

The day I disappeared (page 68)

1 B **2** A **3** D **4** B **5** See below

Explanations

1 This is a **judgement** question. **B** is correct. The story is told in the first person. The *I* and *me* referred to in the story stand for Scotty, the narrator, who is telling a story about something that happened to him. **A** and **C** are incorrect as we only hear comments from Bill and Jo, not the whole story. **D** is incorrect because Mum's voice is not heard in the story.

2 This is a **judgement** question. **A** is correct. Bill and Jo assume Scotty had to leave suddenly for some reason. You can judge that they have very little concern about his disappearance as they don't realise it is a more serious matter than they'd thought. **B, C** and **D** are incorrect as they describe responses that are the opposite of how Scotty's friends reacted.

3 This is a **judgement** question. **D** is correct. Jo doesn't order a hamburger for Scotty when she orders for the others. This makes Scotty realise his friends still don't know he is there. You can judge this is why he decides to sit by himself. **A** is not a reason he would sit by himself at a table. **B** is incorrect because it is clear that Scotty does not want to eat his hamburger alone. **C** is incorrect because Scotty is not afraid of his friends; he just wishes they could see him.

4 This is a **judgement** question. **B** is correct. The story is told in a realistic way as though it is something that actually happens, but in real life people don't disappear in this way. You can judge that the story is a fantasy. **A** is incorrect because something like this could not happen. **C** is likely to be incorrect because science fiction stories are based on science and technology, and there is no evidence of this in the story. **D** is incorrect as, although the story is fiction, it is not connected with historical figures or events.

5 This is a **judgement** question. You may judge that on the whole Scotty takes his own disappearance quite calmly even though he gets miserable and frustrated when others can't see him. He tries to go about things in the usual way and even talks to his bristling, growling dog in a friendly manner.

The advantages and disadvantages of the internet (page 69)

1 D **2** A **3** C **4** B **5** See below

Explanations

1 This is a **judgement** question. **D** is correct. Everyone in Christa's family uses the internet for various purposes. She doesn't report disapproval of it from any member of her family. **A** and **C** are incorrect because both Silver and Paddy report that their parents disapprove of their children spending too much time on the internet. **B** is incorrect because Therese's mother says her boss makes her spend time on the internet when she doesn't want to do so.

2 This is a **judgement** question. **A** is correct. Both Paddy's and Silver's parents complain about their children spending too much time on the internet. **B**, **C** and **D** are incorrect because we are not told what Kara's or Tim's parents think about anything.

3 This is a **judgement** question. **C** is correct. You can judge that Paddy thinks his parents are probably right even though that doesn't make him spend less time on the internet. **A** is incorrect as Paddy says they are probably right. **B** is incorrect as Paddy doesn't express any anger towards them. **D** may be true though this is not clear from what is said. Paddy says the internet has made lessons more fun but he doesn't say what his parents think about its educational value. Their complaint is that he spends too much time on it.

4 This is a **judgement** question. **B** is correct. Tim has two arguments—it saves time and it has programs that counter things like cyberbullying. If you judge that his point about the speed of the internet being an advantage as separate from its saving time, then he makes three arguments in its favour. **A** is incorrect because Christa only has one argument which is that everyone in her family finds the internet useful. **C** is incorrect as Paddy only offers one argument in its favour which is that the internet has improved school lessons. That he likes the internet is a personal view rather than an argument about its advantages. **D** is incorrect as Silver only puts forward one argument—that it allows you to do many different things.

5 This is a **judgement** question. All the children talk about how much they like using the internet, except for Kara. We don't know what Kara thinks as she only mentions a disadvantage of the internet. She may or may not want to be without it. This makes Tim's view, that none of them would like to be without the internet, likely, but not certain, to be accurate. Your own experience with the internet, and how you judge its worth, may influence how accurate you think Tim's prediction is likely to be.

Camouflage in the animal kingdom (page 70)

1 A **2** C **3** C **4** D **5** A **6** See below

Explanations

1 This is a **judgement** question. **A** is correct. This text is about the kinds of camouflage animals use to survive in their environments. You can

judge that this subject makes it suitable for a book about animals and their environments. **B** is incorrect as the text is not about scientific discoveries. **C** is incorrect as the text is not a narrative. **D** is incorrect as the text is too detailed for a young child's picture book.

2 This is a **judgement** question. **C** is correct. The colours of sharks and geckoes are different but each animal's colour matches the colour of the environment in which they live. This helps them camouflage themselves from predators. **A** is incorrect as neither of them use their colouring to frighten predators. **B** is incorrect. They both have shades of grey in their colouring but the shark has bluish tones and the gecko brownish tones. **D** is incorrect as the way their colouring functions in their environments is similar.

3 This is a **judgement** question. **C** is correct. When animals can blend into their surroundings it helps keep them hidden from predators. **A**, **B** and **D** are incorrect as the opposite is true of all of them.

4 This is a **judgement** question. **D** is correct. Hunting is not a camouflage method although camouflage can be used by the predator in the process of hunting. **A** is incorrect because it is a method used in the Arctic by animals who need to blend into different environments. **B** is incorrect as blending into an environment is a key camouflage method used by many animals. **C** is incorrect as it can be useful for animals to appear to be similar to their environments so they escape notice and avoid attack.

5 This is a **judgement** question. **A** is correct. Mimicking the behaviour of its surroundings by keeping still or appearing dead is a useful method of camouflage used by some animals. **C** is incorrect as disturbing its surroundings would draw attention to the animal. **B** is incorrect as striking out when touched will reveal the animal, not conceal it. **D** is incorrect as changing colour repeatedly will make it noticeable and will not help it blend into its environment.

6 This is a **judgement** question. The author's attitude is to accept that there is a law of the jungle and this can't be changed. There is no disapproval expressed even though it is clear that the law of the jungle inevitably leads to death for some.

The clockwork insect (page 71)

1 D **2** C **3** A **4** A **5** See below

Explanations

1 This is a **judgement** question. **D** is correct. Humans thought they were the ones to design gears. To their great surprise they discovered that the same mechanism already existed in nature in the planthopper. **A**, **B** and **C** are all true of a planthopper's gears but they are not what made the discovery of them so surprising.

2 This is a **judgement** question. **C** is correct. The text reports the news of a scientific discovery. It is written in a way that is not highly technical but gives interesting information. **A** is incorrect as a reader would expect to read about the activities of staff and students in a school newsletter. **B** is incorrect as the text is not in comic format. **D** is incorrect as the text includes the author's opinion (*We are learning …*) *(see line 30)* and it is not a complete summary of a particular topic as you would expect to find in a Wikipedia entry.

3 This is a **judgement** question. **A** is correct. The author is full of enthusiasm for what has been discovered and what this might lead to in the future. **B** is incorrect because the author doesn't express any disappointment about the discovery. **C** is incorrect because the author's attitude is the opposite of unenthusiastic. **D** is incorrect as the author doesn't express any concerns about the discovery.

4 This is a **judgement** question. **A** is correct. You can judge that the author wants the reader to see with their own eyes how the tops of the teeth on the planthopper's legs are structured and work like gears. **B** is incorrect because although the diagram is of the mechanism a planthopper uses to jump, it doesn't show how far it can jump. **C** may be true but it is not the main reason the author includes the diagram. **D** is incorrect. There is no scale included on the diagram to indicate a planthopper's size, but pointing out its size is not its main purpose.

5 This is a **judgement** question. You may judge from the evidence in the text that scientists now realise the animal kingdom may have many more secrets for them to uncover. It means human researchers are realising that they can learn more from the animal kingdom than they previously thought they could.

Anthony Browne's *King Kong* (page 72)

1 B **2** C **3** B **4** B **5** See below

Explanations

1 This is a **judgement** question. **B** is correct. Edgar and Cooper disagree on everything except for Cooper agreeing that the action makes the book exciting. **A** is incorrect as Edgar and Cooper hardly agree on anything. **C** is incorrect as Edgar and Cooper have only one similar opinion. **D** is incorrect: there is one thing they agree on—that the action makes the book exciting.

2 This is a **judgement** question. **C** is correct. Cooper argues that the book is *over the top* *(see line 4)* and unbelievable. He remains unconvinced by most of Edgar's arguments in favour of the book. His review would be fairly critical. **A**, **B** and **D** are incorrect as Cooper has nothing complimentary to say about the book in the discussion.

3 This is a **judgement** question. **B** is correct because Edgar has good arguments to support his view of the book and these counter Cooper's views. He understands how authors make you feel for characters and what happens to them. He appreciates how illustrations work with the text to create its meanings. **A** is incorrect because just having a different view from Cooper's does not make his view convincing. **C** is incorrect as liking the book is not what makes his opinion convincing. **D** is incorrect because the number of words he uses has nothing to do with the strength of his arguments.

4 This is a **judgement** question. **B** is correct. Edgar knows there are several versions of the movie and he knows their dates and who acted in them. **A** is incorrect as there is no evidence that Cooper has seen the 1933 version of the movie. **C** is incorrect as there is no evidence that Cooper is not a good judge of movies. **D** may be true but there isn't any strong evidence for this. All Edgar's comments are closely related to points raised by the discussion so don't seem to be made to show off.

5 This is a **judgement** question. Cooper does not express his point of view very convincingly. The reasons he gives for not liking the book, *King Kong*, suggest he doesn't understand it is a fantasy, as Edgar points out. Cooper doesn't give any reason for preferring the film to the book and reveals he doesn't know as much as Edgar does about it.

The Rainbow Dragon's Lair (page 73)

1 C **2** D **3** B **4** A **5** See below

Explanations

1 This is a **judgement** question. **C** is correct. You can judge from the title and the narrative that this text is from a story about two fictional characters, Willa and the Rainbow Dragon. **A** is incorrect as it is a story, not an interview. No questions are asked and the only words said are recited by Willa. **B** is incorrect because dragons are not real and the text tells a story rather than giving an account of how dragons behave. **D** is incorrect because although the text tells a story it is not well known and it is not in the form of a fairy tale.

2 This is a **judgement** question. **D** is correct. The atmosphere is the mood that the author creates. It changes from the calm of the opening to the dramatic tension in paragraph two as the reader sees Willa at the mercy of the dragon. **A**, **B** and **C** are incorrect because they describe atmospheres that don't account for the fear and danger of the moment for Willa.

3 This is a **judgement** question. **B** is correct. The dragon is described as being *ready for the kill* *(see line 8)* which suggests that being good natured is not one of his qualities. **A** is incorrect because we know the dragon likes to sleep in the day. He is doing that (looking like a quilt) when Willa enters his cave. **C** is incorrect as we are told of the dragon's roar that petrifies Willa. **D** is incorrect because we learn the dragon has stolen treasure from Willa's family in the past.

4 This is a **judgement** question. **A** is correct. Willa is frightened of the dragon and yet she continues to challenge him. She knows she must get back the family treasure or her family will starve. **B** is incorrect because Willa's actions are the opposite of cowardly and weak. **C** is incorrect as although Willa acts desperately, her actions can't be described as evil. **D** is incorrect as it is uncertain how wise Willa's actions are. She acts hopefully rather than confidently.

5 This is a **judgement** question. You may judge it is likely that Willa will escape as charms usually work for heroines in stories. There is evidence that the charm has already had a powerful effect on the dragon. It also seems likely Willa will find a way to rescue the treasure because it is so important to her that she save her family from starving to death.

That it is a waste of money to develop robots (page 74)

1 A **2** D **3** D **4** C **5** See below

Explanations

1 This is a **judgement** question. **A** is correct. Kent asks the question not to find an answer but to make the point that the research was a waste of money. You can judge Kent is suggesting the research found out something that could have been found out without spending all that time and money. **B** is incorrect because Kent does not think a robotic squirrel is at all helpful. **C** is incorrect because he is already convinced that robotic squirrels are unnecessary. **D** is incorrect because Kent thinks he knows better than the researchers.

2 This is a **judgement** question. **D** is correct as this is the only sentence that mentions a benefit (education) that Kent implies might be worthwhile if it were less expensive. **A** is a statement giving information but it is not an argument. **B** is incorrect as it is critical of making something very expensive simply to entertain people. **C** is incorrect as in the context the question implies it was not worth the huge investment.

3 This is a **judgement** question. **D** is correct. That developing robots is not cost effective is the only sentence that supports Kent's view that it is a waste of money to develop robots. **A**, **B** and **C** are incorrect as they all point out important ways robots can improve human life that could make it worthwhile to invest in their development.

4 This is a **judgement** question. **C** is correct. You can judge that the facts Kent uses are taken from his research and there is no evidence that he makes them up. **A**, **B** and **D** are all ways he presents his arguments. He uses examples to support his point of view; he argues persuasively and builds towards a conclusion, that as far as he can tell research into robots is wasteful.

5 This is a **judgement** question. You may judge that Kent makes some good points but his view as a whole is not very convincing. He doesn't mention many of the ways robots can benefit society. He doesn't go fully into their educational possibilities or discuss their use in war, their help for people with disabilities or the way they can do boring or dangerous tasks to help humans. Research into their development could also lead to new understandings about humans.

Could it have happened? (page 75)

1 C **2** C **3** B **4** D **5** See below

Explanations

1 This is a **judgement** question. **C** is correct. You can judge that the use of informal language such as calling an Australian kangaroo an *Aussie roo* (see line 20) and using an expression such as *That's nothing new* (see line 31) are examples of the informal language likely to be used in a newspaper article rather than a history text. **A** is incorrect because the words *Dutch* and *Portuguese* could appear in either a newspaper article or a history text. **B** is incorrect because although some of the language is fairly formal there is also informal language included (see **C** above). **D** is incorrect because either kind of publication could include ideas.

2 This is a **judgement** question. **C** is correct. You can judge the *it* in the title stands for the idea that the Portuguese may have reached Australia before the Dutch voyage of 1606. **A** is incorrect because *it* does not stand for the Portuguese seeing Aussie roos, but whether they saw them before 1606. **B** is incorrect because *it* does not stand for the idea that the English came to Australia first. The text implies the English arrived after the Dutch. **D** is incorrect because *it* does not stand for the idea that the Dutch came to Australia before the Portuguese, but rather that the reverse may have happened.

3 This is a **judgement** question. **B** is correct. You can judge the image could be a kangaroo but it could also be the drawing of a different animal that looks like a kangaroo. **A** is incorrect as there is no evidence in the text that the drawing

is unclear. **C** is incorrect because the text does not suggest all kangaroos look the same. **D** is incorrect because the Portuguese word for kangaroo is not relevant to doubt about the image being a kangaroo.

4 This is a **judgement** question. **D** is correct. You can judge the picture does not prove the present view of what happened in history is wrong, though if further evidence is found then its discovery may possibly help to rewrite history. **A**, **B** and **C** are incorrect because they all express certainty of some kind and nothing has yet been proven.

5 This is a **judgement** question. You may judge the sentence *That's nothing new though—it happens all the time* (see lines 32–33) suggests that our understanding of what happened in the past is forever changing. This is because we are always discovering things we haven't known or understood fully before.

Mixed questions

How is glass made? (page 76)

1 C **2** A **3** C **4** D **5** B **6** See below

Explanations

1 This is a **fact-finding** question. **C** is correct. The answer is stated directly in the text. The sand is turned into a *glassy substance called obsidian* (see line 5) by the heat of the lava. **A**, **B** and **D** are incorrect as a glassy substance is formed, not earth, more sand or lava.

2 This is a **fact-finding** question. **A** is correct. The answer is stated directly in the text. The text says when sodium ash and limestone are added to sand *they lower its melting point* (see line 8). **B** is incorrect because the reason for adding sodium ash and limestone to sand is not to double its quantity. **C** is incorrect because it is adding minerals such as cobalt or sulphur that colours the glass, not sodium ash and limestone. **D** is incorrect because the melting point needs to be lowered, not raised, to make sand.

3 This is a **language** question. **C** is correct. The numbers are measurements of temperature using different scales. The brackets mean that 3092 °F (Fahrenheit) is the equivalent of, or the same as, 1700 °C (Celsius). **A**, **B** and **D** are incorrect because the brackets are used to show that the temperatures on the different scales are equal, not hotter or cooler.

4 This is an **inferring** question. **D** is correct. You can infer that workers dealing with hot liquids are at risk of serious injury from high heat so they wear protective clothing. **A** is incorrect as workers would be warm already from being close to high temperatures; protective clothing would make them even warmer. **B** is incorrect as clothing doesn't protect the furnace, it protects the workers. **C** is incorrect as this isn't the reason they wear the clothing, although it may have the effect of warning others to keep away.

5 This is a **language** question. **B** is correct. The word *myriad* (see line 15) means 'many' in this context. When you think about the different uses for glass you know there are many not listed here. This means *myriad* must mean a number greater than a few, one or two (**A** or **D**) but it would not mean as many as trillions (**C**). **A**, **C** and **D** are incorrect for the reasons described above.

6 This is a **language** question. The words *endlessly 100% recyclable* (see line 17) mean 'can be used over and over again'.

Ratty times (page 77)

1 D **2** B **3** B **4** D **5** C **6** See below

Explanations

1 This is an **inferring** question. **D** is correct. Mrs Rat refers to Harold as the big brother of her new litter, which makes him her son. **A** is incorrect as Cape Town is the name of a city and a port. **B** and **C** are incorrect as they are names for Mrs Rat's husband.

2 This is a **synthesis** question. **B** is correct. The stage directions in this script instruct the actors how to say their lines: Mr Rat is to sound wistful; Mrs Rat is to use a shrill voice to express her annoyance; and the unseen female convict is to screech piercingly. **A** is incorrect as these stage directions don't tell the characters how to move. **C** is incorrect as these stage directions are not about lighting. **D** is incorrect as these stage directions don't tell the characters when the lines are to be said.

3 This is a **synthesis** question. **B** is correct. Mrs Rat is irritable as she complains crossly about

everything, while Mr Rat is calmer and more even tempered. **A** is incorrect because there is no evidence of Mrs Rat behaving calmly or of Mr Rat behaving irritably. **C** is incorrect because there is no evidence of Mrs Rat behaving in an easy-going way. **D** is incorrect because there is no evidence of Mr Rat acting in an unkind way.

4 This is an **inferring** question. **D** is correct. You can infer that when Mrs Rat hears the female convict's screech she guesses Harold has frightened her. She is relieved to have found him at last so says *Ah, thank goodness (see line 19)*. **A** and **C** are incorrect because while they may be true they are not the reason Mrs Rat says *Ah, thank goodness*. **B** is incorrect because there is no evidence Mr Rat passes her a lump of cheese.

5 This is a **judgement** question. **C** is correct. You can judge the author gives the rats human qualities such as being able to talk, have family problems and show emotion. **A** is incorrect because the author shows the rats' behaviour to be far from perfect. **B** is incorrect because while some of their actions earn disapproval, the author shows rats have their problems like anyone else. **D** is incorrect because Mrs Rat already stands up for her rights.

6 This is an **inferring** question. Evidence in the text shows:
- it was a long sea voyage taking more than 240 days
- it left from Portsmouth in 1787
- it stopped briefly in Capetown for supplies in October, 1787
- there were convicts on board.

These details suggest it was a convict ship heading south and possibly for Botany Bay, Australia. If you know about the first fleet voyage to Botany Bay you will see that the dates and route described match it exactly. You might also know that black rats were introduced to Australia from the first fleet.

Woollarawarre Bennelong (c.1764–1813) (page 78)

1 B **2** D **3** A **4** D **5** C **6** See below

Explanations

1 This is a **fact-finding** question. The answer is stated directly in the text. **B** is correct. *Muting* is the Eora name for spear. In the text the word has its English meaning placed after it in brackets. **A**, **C** and **D** are incorrect because they name things that are not meanings for the word *muting*.

2 This is a **language** question. **D** is correct because HMS *Reliance* is English. **A**, **B** and **C** are incorrect as they are all Eora words, making **D** the odd one out.

3 This is an **inferring** question. **A** is correct. You can infer that Bennelong would not have had a birth certificate. His birth year has been worked out as around 1764 from guesses made of his age at the time of the first settlement. His death date is recorded accurately. **B** is incorrect because the c. before the date doesn't mean it is an important date; it is an estimate or guess of when he was born. **C** is incorrect because the author would never have found a correct date as it is not recorded. **D** is incorrect because the author is not drawing attention to his birth date but showing it may not be accurate as there are no records of it.

4 This is an **inferring** question. **D** is correct. It was named after Bennelong, who lived there for a time. **A** is incorrect as there is no evidence Bennelong asked for the point to be named after him and unlikely that he would do so. **B** may be true but it is not the reason Bennelong Point has that name. **C** is incorrect as there is no evidence that the name used by the Eora peoples was difficult to say.

5 This is a **synthesis** question. **C** is correct. The text gives a brief overview of Bennelong's life from his birth to his death. **A** is incorrect as the problem faced by Governor Philip is only a part of Bennelong's life story. **B** is incorrect as the information about First Australians' life relates particularly to Bennelong and is not a general account of the First Australian way of life. **D** is incorrect because the text does not describe the English way of life.

6 This is a **judgement** question. You may judge from evidence in the text that the relationship between Governor Philip and Bennelong improved over time. At first Bennelong was Governor Philip's kidnapped prisoner but as time went on:
- Bennelong moved into Governor Philip's house
- Governor Philip built Bennelong a brick hut in a place of Bennelong's choice

- Bennelong acted as an interpreter and go-between for Governor Philip
- Governor Philip took Bennelong to England with him.

The Wonderful Wizard of Oz (page 79)

1 C **2** B **3** D **4** D **5** A **6** See below

Explanations

1 This is a **fact-finding** question. The answer is stated directly in the text. **C** is correct. Dorothy and Uncle Henry heard *a low wail of the wind* (see line 2). **A** is incorrect as Aunt Em screams and does not wail. **B** is incorrect because Toto doesn't make a sound. **D** is incorrect because the text says it was the wind that wailed, not the grass.

2 This is a **language** question. **B** is correct. The wind forces the long grass downwards so it looks as if it is bowing. **A** is incorrect as there is no evidence that the wind is welcoming the storm. **C** and **D** are incorrect because *bow* means 'bend downwards'. It doesn't mean 'bend in all directions' or 'stand upright'.

3 This is a **judgement** question. **D** is correct. You can judge that Uncle Henry's reaction is to show concern for others when he immediately warns his wife of the coming storm and rushes to look after his animals. You can judge that Dorothy's reaction is to show concern for Toto when she chases after him rather than first trying to save herself. **A** is incorrect as neither Uncle Henry nor Dorothy complain. **B** is incorrect as neither Uncle Henry nor Dorothy hide. **C** is incorrect as only Dorothy decides to hide but firstly she tries to catch Toto to keep him safe.

4 This is a **synthesis** question. **D** is correct. Uncle Henry runs to the sheds to look after the animals; Dorothy plans to go to the cellar with Toto but she falls down before she gets there. It is only Aunt Em who has time to climb down the ladder before the cyclone whirls the house away. **A** is incorrect as they all knew about the cellar. **B** is incorrect because the others did not choose other hiding places. **C** is incorrect because although Toto hides under the bed he is rescued by Dorothy, who is prevented from getting to the cellar by the cyclone knocking her down.

5 This is a **synthesis** question. **A** is correct. Everything in the text is about the coming of the cyclone and how it affects the family. **B** is incorrect because Toto doesn't get lost and his activities are only part of the story. **C** is incorrect because Dorothy doesn't go up in a balloon and the balloon is only referred to in the last line. **D** is incorrect as there may well be danger ahead but that isn't what this part of the story is about.

6 This is a **judgement** question. You may judge the atmosphere changes from anxiety and fear to one where it feels as if something unexpected, and possibly exciting, is about to happen. The single-sentence paragraph *(Then a strange thing happened.)* (see line 17) after the long paragraph of frantic activity alters the pace of the story, slowing it down. Then when the house rises *slowly through the air* and Dorothy feels *as if she were going up in a balloon* (see lines 18–19) things begin to sound strange and interesting rather than terrifying.

Talking about books (page 80)

1 D **2** B **3** C **4** A **5** D **6** See below

Explanations

1 This is a **fact-finding** question. **D** is correct. The answer is stated directly in the text. You read that Fabiano says *Want some grapes?* (see line 3) and Gazz says *These grapes are great* (see line 12). **A**, **B** and **C** are incorrect as they do not eat any of those foods. They do talk about chocolate and peach but they don't eat them.

2 This is a **synthesis** question. **B** is correct. Two boys are talking about books in a relaxed, casual way. **A** is incorrect as they are not in a classroom and there is nothing formal about the way the boys express their ideas. **C** is incorrect as no-one is being questioned in an official way. The boys are just talking naturally to each other exchanging their opinions. **D** is incorrect as the boys are talking to each other, not to a radio audience.

3 This is a **synthesis** question. **C** is correct. The *revolting* kids in *Charlie and the Chocolate Factory* and the *cruel aunts, Sponge and Spiker* (see line 14), in *James and the Giant Peach* are nasty characters. **A** is incorrect because only Charlie lives with his parents; James's parents are dead. **B** is incorrect as Quentin is the first name of the illustrator of both books. He is

not a character in them. **D** is incorrect because although James has lost his parents, Charlie Bucket hasn't.

4 This is a **judgement** question. **A** is correct. Both boys praise the way Blake does his drawings for the books, which is a way of admiring them. You can judge that although Fabiano says they look scribbled, he thinks this is part of what makes them so good. **B** may be true but neither boy expresses envy of Blake's talent, only admiration. **C** and **D** are incorrect as the boys' attitude is the opposite of unimpressed and disrespectful.

5 This is a **language** question. **D** is correct. The words *gets you in* (see line 13) here mean get you interested, draw you into the story. **A** is incorrect because Fabiano says the opposite of this; he means it makes you want to read it because of the way it is written. **B** is incorrect because the word *in* does not mean indoors in this expression. It is part of the expression *gets you in*, meaning 'captures your interest'. **C** is incorrect because you are not drawn into the book by being tricked or deceived.

6 This is a **synthesis** question. You can connect information from the text to see that it seems likely Gazz would read the book for several reasons:
   - He says it sounds like a good book.
   - He is very enthusiastic about another Roald Dahl book.
   - Fabiano recommends it and thinks he would like it.

The age of discovery (page 81)

1 B **2** B **3** B **4** C **5** C **6** See below

Explanations

1 This is a **fact-finding** question. **B** is correct. The answer is stated directly in the text. You read *In 1522 Magellan led a successful sailing expedition around the world* (see line 4). **A**, **C** and **D** are incorrect because they name dates when Magellan did not sail around the world.

2 This is a **fact-finding** question. **B** is correct. The answer is stated directly in the text. You read *His journeys* [Magellan's sailing expedition] *proved to Europeans that the world was not flat* (see lines 4–5). **A** is incorrect because Europeans were unaware of Australia at that time. **C** and **D** are incorrect because Magellan's and Columbus's voyages are not compared in terms of who was the better sailor.

3 This is an **inferring** question. **B** is correct. You can infer that Columbus was on a voyage of discovery and the Americas were new to him and other Europeans. **A** and **C** are incorrect as the Americas were not new to the indigenous people as they already lived there. **D** is incorrect as there were indigenous people living in the Americas.

4 This is a **synthesis** question. **C** is correct. The text as a whole gives a brief account of the causes and patterns of European colonisation between the 16th and 18th centuries. **A** is incorrect because the text is only partly about Columbus and Magellan. There is much more about the consequences of their journeys than about them. **B** is incorrect because only the last paragraph is about James Cook. **D** is incorrect because the 10th to the 12th century was long before the events that are outlined.

5 This is a **judgement** question. **C** is correct. You can judge that indigenous peoples are reported on by others but their own views are not mentioned. **A** is incorrect as it is clear that the Spanish rulers supported the idea of expanding their empire and seeking wealth and power. **B** is incorrect as map makers were recorders of the discoveries and did not express views about them. **D** is incorrect. The sample of a Dutch navigator's view that is in the text is similar to that of other views.

6 This is a **judgement** question. You may judge that they were not looking at exactly the same places or peoples. Carstensz was looking at the northern coast and Cook at the eastern coast of Australia. These were different landscapes inhabited by different First Australian peoples. It also seems likely that the values and attitudes of the two men were different. They thought about what they saw in different ways.

Should you feed wild birds? (2) (page 82)

1 B **2** C **3** A, B and C **4** D **5** A
6 See below

Explanations

1 This is a **synthesis** question. **B** is correct. Felix puts the case for feeding wild birds and explains how to do it so birds are protected

from harm. **A** is incorrect as he doesn't describe the pleasures it brings. **C** is incorrect as the text is about Felix's view and, while he refers to Marissa's view, he doesn't discuss other views. **D** is incorrect because although Felix reports on some research he doesn't discuss current research in the text.

2 This is an **inferring** question. **C** is correct. Felix implies that he disapproves of having birds in cages when he says feeding wild birds is *much better than having birds in cages!* (see line 4). **A** is incorrect as following a feeding routine is supported by Felix in his rules. **B** is incorrect as Felix approves of feeding wild birds. **D** is incorrect as Felix doesn't disapprove of research; he quotes it in support of his own opinion.

3 This is a **fact-finding** question. **A**, **B** and **C** are correct. The answers are stated directly in the text. Felix says *Do not feed them sugar, honey, bread or processed foods* (see line 14). **D** is incorrect as Felix says feeding wild birdseed can be helpful.

4 This is an **inferring** question. **D** is correct. You can infer that making birds dependent on humans for their food is a reason against feeding them. It makes them unable to survive in their natural environment. **A**, **B** and **C** are incorrect as they are all reasons that support the feeding of wild birds.

5 This is a **language** question. **A** is correct. When Felix says *go for it!* (see line 20) he is lending his support to the idea that it is good to feed birds if you do it in the correct way. **B** is incorrect because Felix is not encouraging the reader to visit anywhere. **C** is incorrect because Felix does not suggest doing more research. **D** is not what Felix suggests. Your own feelings could be the opposite of what Felix says.

6 This is a **judgement** question. You may judge that this is a class debate and so you can't tell what Felix's actual beliefs are. He may have been assigned the positive case on a class topic and had no choice but to defend the topic question. His speech expresses care about the environment. He states he is concerned about the welfare of native birds. He has undertaken research and written a set of rules to share his knowledge. But we don't know if this is genuine or simply for the classroom task.

My trip to China (page 83)

1 B and D **2** A **3** C **4** D **5** B
6 See below

Explanations

1 This is a **fact-finding** question. **B** and **D** are correct. The answers are stated directly in the text. Theo says *My next ambition is to travel to Hangzhou* and *I'm hoping to see ... the Island to Remind You of Your Childhood* (see lines 16–18). **A** is incorrect as Theo says *My travels have brought me to Beijing* (see lines 5–6). **C** is incorrect because Theo says *I'm just back from seeing the Great Wall of China* (see lines 11–12).

2 This is an **inferring** question. **A** is correct. Theo's host says *sandstorms come from the northern deserts and are troublesome for people and the environment* (see lines 8–10). You can infer sandstorms affect people's health and spoil their farmlands. **B** is incorrect because while it is true they come from the north, this is not what makes the sandstorms themselves so troublesome. **C** may be true but the sandstorms are more than a nuisance; they are troublesome in particular ways. **D** is not a reason for sandstorms being troublesome.

3 This is a **fact-finding** question. **C** is correct. The answer is stated directly in the text. Theo compares the Great Wall to a dragon when he says *It's like a long dragon winding its way through the landscape* (see lines 12–13). **A** and **B** are incorrect as Theo makes no comparison between the Great Wall and either a monkey or a pathway. **D** is incorrect because he says part of the Great Wall is in ruins, not that it is like ruins.

4 This is a **judgement** question. **D** is correct. You can judge that the way Theo writes to his sister shows he thinks of her affectionately and has a strong bond with her. **A** is incorrect as Theo's tone is warm and friendly towards his little sister, rather than cool or distant. **B** is incorrect as although Theo teases his little sister, he never orders her about. **C** is incorrect as there is no sign that he is cross or feels annoyed with his sister in his email.

5 This is a **language** question. **B** is correct. The government flooded the cities with water, which is a kind of drowning, to make a dam. This is why the word *'drowned'* (see line 19)

is in inverted commas as only people can be drowned, not cities. **A** is true but it is not what the quoted words mean. **C** is incorrect as the cities died an unnatural or artificial death as they were '*drowned*' by the government. **D** is incorrect as the cities were not moved but left where they were.

6 This is a **synthesis** question. Theo uses the internet in several ways:
   - He sends an email via the internet.
   - He uses an emoticon :) in his email to send a smile in internet language.
   - He uses the word *google* (see line 21) in a way that suggests he is used to using the internet to search for information.

The Ugly Animal Preservation Society (page 84)

1 A **2** C **3** D **4** D **5** A **6** See below

Explanations

1 This is a **fact-finding** question. **A** is correct. The answer is stated directly in the text. Chloe asks *Which animal won?* and Ben answers *It was the blobfish.* (see lines 14–15). **B**, **C** and **D** name animals that did not win the competition.

2 This is a **judgement** question. **C** is correct. Chloe says *I vote we start a branch of the society* and Ben replies *Yes! Let's set up a blog and invite all our friends to choose an animal for* our *mascot* (see lines 31–35). Both Ben and Chloe are showing their enthusiasm for the society and what it does. **A**, **B** and **D** are incorrect because they describe attitudes that are the opposite of the attitude Ben and Chloe have towards the society. They show great interest in the society and its work and even want to set up their own branch.

3 This is an **inferring** question. **D** is correct. You can read between the lines that the blobfish makes a good mascot because it is a symbol for other animals that need protection. This is because people think they are ugly or unattractive. **A**, **B** and **C** describe features of the blobfish, rather than explain why it makes a good mascot for the society.

4 This is a **synthesis** question. **D** is correct because, until the society was formed, none of the events named had happened. **A** is incorrect because Ben and Chloe only planned to set up a blog after the original society was formed. **B** and **C** are incorrect because the competition was held after the society was set up.

5 This is a **language** question. **A** is correct. When Chloe says *You're on* (see line 36) she means she agrees with Ben's ideas and wants to work with him on them. **B** is incorrect because when Chloe says *You're on* she doesn't mean Ben should follow his ideas by himself, but that they should do it together. **C** is incorrect because when Chloe says *You're on* she implies she wants to be part of the things Ben suggests doing. **D** is incorrect because it is already understood that Ben is part of their society.

6 This is a **judgement** question. You may judge the blobfish is unfortunate because people find it very ugly to look at. Also as they are not a protected species they are often caught in fishing nets, which has reduced their numbers. On the other hand now that people are raising awareness about the blobfish you may judge that its fortunes are improving and that it is quite lucky to have notice taken of it.

Barangaroo (page 85)

1 D **2** C **3** B **4** C **5** See below

Explanations

1 This is a **fact-finding** question. **D** is correct. The answer is stated directly in the text. Barangaroo belonged to the *Cammeraygal* nation (see line 3). **A** is incorrect as Bennelong was the name of her husband. **B** is incorrect as Dilboong was the name of her daughter. **C** is incorrect as Wangal was not the name of her nation.

2 This is a **fact-finding** question. **C** is correct. The answer is stated directly in the text. Barangaroo *chose to stay with her own people instead* [of living with Bennelong and the English at Governor Philip's house] (see lines 6–7). **A** is incorrect as the text says she could have lived there if she had wanted to do so. **B** is incorrect as there is no evidence of Bennelong not wanting her at Governor Philip's house. **D** is incorrect as there is no evidence of what her clan thought about the idea of her living at Governor Philip's house.

3 This is an **inferring** question. **B** is correct. You can infer that the Cammeraygal people did not keep written records. We are not told her birth date because it is not known or recorded

anywhere. **A** is incorrect as Barangaroo did not have a birth certificate of the kind Europeans have. **C** is incorrect because there is no known date that could be copied. **D** is incorrect because Barangaroo did not know that a biography would ever be written about her.

4 This is a **judgement** question. **C** is correct. You can judge it was part of Barangaroo's way of life not to wear clothes so it is unlikely she would enjoy shopping for clothes. **A** is incorrect. The text says that Barangaroo followed the customs of her people and was courageous so it is likely she would have some spear wounds on her body. **B** is incorrect. The text shows that she had courage and did what she thought was the right thing so it is likely she would threaten someone doing what she saw as wrong. **D** is incorrect. The text shows Barangaroo as strong minded and far from timid so it is likely she stood up to Bennelong when she was angry.

5 This is a **judgement** question. You can judge that Barangaroo did what she thought was right in spite of pressure to change her ways. For example, she lived with her own people instead of moving to the Governor's house when invited; she would not accept drink when dining at the house; and she did not copy European ways of dressing but kept to her own customs.

Marianne Musgrove's *The Worry Tree* (page 86)

1 C **2** A **3** D **4** C **5** A **6** See below

Explanations

1 This is a **fact-finding** question. **C** is correct. The answer is stated directly in the text. *The Worry Tree* is written by Marianne Musgrove. **A**, **B** and **D** are incorrect as they are not the author's first name.

2 This is an **inferring** question. **A** is correct. You can infer from the text that Juliet *worries about everything you can think of* (see lines 5–6). She is called a *worrywart* for this reason. **B**, **C** and **D** are incorrect as we are not told that Juliet has any of these ailments.

3 This is a **synthesis** question. **D** is correct. The main purpose of the text is to review the book by analysing who it is for, what it is about and how well it is written. **A** is incorrect. The text refers to parts of the story but this is not its main purpose. **B** is incorrect. The text describes some of the characters but this is not its main purpose. **C** is incorrect. The text emphasises the good qualities of the book but not in order to advertise it.

4 This is a **fact-finding** question. **C** is correct. The answer is stated directly in the text. The text says Juliet found the Worry Tree *painted on the wall beneath some peeling wallpaper* (see lines 17–18). **A** is incorrect because the tree is not alive. **B** is incorrect because it is there on the wall and is not imagined (although Juliet may imagine things about what it can do.) **D** is incorrect because the tree has been painted on the wall so it is not a photo of a tree.

5 This is a **judgement** question. **A** is correct. You can judge that the author praises the book for several different reasons and concludes that it is a *must read* (see line 23). **B** is incorrect because there are no criticisms of the book in the text. **C** is incorrect because the author says the book is about the kind of problems *that concern most boys and girls* (see lines 7–8) which suggests that boys will be interested in the book. **D** is incorrect because all the comments about the book are positive.

6 This is a **judgement** question. Your judgement about the usefulness of a Worry Tree will depend on the kind of problems you experience. It also may depend on whether you think imagining someone else looking after your problems is a useful way to deal with them.

New Year's resolutions (page 87)

1 B **2** C **3** C **4** D **5** B **6** See below

Explanations

1 This is a **judgement** question. **B** is correct. You can judge that Danny talks to his diary as though it were a close friend and tells it things he feels he can't tell other people. **A** is incorrect as Danny tells his diary his secret thoughts. **C** and **D** are incorrect because Danny says he doesn't think he should tell these thoughts to *them* (see line 9), which includes his brother and Aunt Jessica.

2 This is an **inferring** question. **C** is correct. You can infer that Ms Jenkins is Danny's teacher and not a family member. This is because he calls her Ms Jenkins and she finds spelling mistakes

in his stories. **A** is incorrect as some of the others (his mum, sister and Aunt Jessica) are female. **B** is incorrect as everyone in Danny's list knows him. **D** is incorrect because Danny's dad also points out mistakes made by Danny.

3 This is a **language** question. **C** is correct. Danny repeats the word to emphasise that he wants his brother to be kept in his room for a very long time. It is a way of showing that at times he gets very annoyed with his brother. **A** and **D** are incorrect because it is not written for either his brother or mother to read. **B** is incorrect because repeating the word *hours* *(see lines 11–12)* has nothing to do with his mother wasting time.

4 This is an **inferring** question. **D** is correct. You can infer that his baby brother is too small to know how to promise anything so he could not make any New Year's resolutions. **A**, **B** and **C** are incorrect as it is not absolutely certain that these family members won't make these New Year's resolutions, even though it is unlikely.

5 This is an **inferring** question. **B** is correct. You can infer that Danny's big sister won't believe him because he says she is always telling him *she's better than I am at football and cricket* *(see lines 17–18)*. **A** is incorrect as there is no evidence in the text that Aunt Jessica has spoken about this to Danny. **C** is incorrect because the text that says Danny thinks he is better than his big sister. **D** is incorrect as there is no evidence that his sister is a bully.

6 This is a **judgement** question. Answers will vary. You need to look for clues, such as how intensely Danny expresses his feelings and which resolutions are about things that happen all the time.

Come to the Alice (page 88)

1 C **2** B **3** B **4** A **5** B **6** See below

Explanations

1 This is a **synthesis** question. **C** is correct. Everything in the text is there to persuade families to visit the Alice for a holiday. **A** is incorrect as visiting Uluru is one of several activities named to persuade families to visit Alice Springs. **B** is incorrect because the text does not persuade everyone to change their minds, just those who think they would not enjoy the Alice. **D** is incorrect because thinking about holiday activities is a technique used to persuade the reader to visit the Alice, not just to have a holiday anywhere.

2 This is a **language** question. **B** is correct. The text persuades families to visit the Alice. It repeats the word *family* three times and gives reasons why the whole family would enjoy the Alice. **A**, **C** and **D** are incorrect because although young children, teenagers and adults may be a part of a family, the text does not try to persuade these groups specifically to visit the Alice.

3 This is a **synthesis** question. **B** is correct. The activities include unusual things such as camel riding and hot-air ballooning. **A** and **D** are incorrect as they are not typical of activities always on offer. **C** is incorrect because the activities are a mix of physical (e.g. bike riding, swimming) and mental activities (e.g. listening, watching).

4 This is a **language** question. **A** is correct. Adjectives that are used to describe parts of the landscape are *beautiful, swaying, ancient, tropical* and *stunning* *(see lines 12–14)*. In the context these sound inviting and attractive. **B** is incorrect because the words used do not suggest an arid, bare place. **C** is incorrect because while the word 'ancient' adds a touch of history, the word 'worn out' does not apply to any part of the landscape that is described. **D** is possibly true of the landscape of the Alice but these aspects are not emphasised.

5 This is a **judgement** question. **B** is correct. You can judge that the Alice is described as *set in the heart of history* *(see line 7)* because it is placed where the first Australians lived for thousands of years of their history. **A** is incorrect because although the Alice is roughly in the centre of Australia, this is only part of the reason it is described as being *set in the heart of history*. **C** is true but it is not a reason for the Alice to be described as *set in the heart of history*. **D** is incorrect because being a great place to visit does not explain why it is described as *set in the heart of history*.

6 This is a **judgement** question. You may judge that the words used by the YOU in the text suggest a person who is
- part of a family
- knows how to use Aussie slang
- can be persuaded to change his or her mind
- is attracted to adventure.

Idioms (page 89)

1 A **2** B **3** D **4** C **5** A **6** See below

Explanations

1 This is a **language** question. **A** is correct. You read *English has over 25 000 expressions of this kind* [idioms] *(see lines 3–4)*. The word *over* means 'more than' in this context. **B** and **C** are incorrect as their numbers do not match what is said in the text. **D** is incorrect because the text says people have *estimated (see line 3)* the number.

2 This is a **language** question. **B** is correct. The phrase *each individual word (see line 13)* means each word thought about as though it were separate from any other word. **A** is incorrect because the idea of words being together is the opposite of what this phrase means. **C** and **D** are incorrect because the meaning of the phrase does not include the idea of difficulty or of having personality.

3 This is an **inferring** question. **D** is correct. You can infer that idioms don't spoil the language as the text says they enrich it: *Idioms enrich the language and give it its own special character (see lines 4–5)*. **A**, **B** and **C** describe idioms accurately, which makes them incorrect.

4 This is an **inferring** question. **C** is correct. You read *What these groups of words* [idioms] *literally mean doesn't make much sense (see lines 14–15)*. You can infer that if they don't make sense literally, then they have meanings that can't be understood literally. **A** is incorrect as idioms do make sense. **B** is incorrect because idioms keep their meaning when in a sentence. **D** is incorrect because idioms have meanings that people understand.

5 This is a **synthesis** question. **A** is correct. The idiom *to cost an arm and a leg (see line 8)* is a statement used to show that the literal meaning of this sentence doesn't make sense. It is not usual to pay for things with body parts! **B** is incorrect because it is the opposite of **A**. **C** is a general statement about people's use of language and not why this idiom is used in the text. **D** is incorrect because the idiom is used to prove something about idioms, not about statements that are literally true.

6 This is a **synthesis** question. You learn from the text that idioms can be difficult for new language learners to understand. This is because as they learn a new vocabulary they learn what words literally mean but when they find the words used as part of an idiom they have to learn to think about their meanings in a different way.

Huon pine (page 90)

1 B **2** D **3** A **4** C **5** B and D
6 See below

Explanations

1 This is a **fact-finding** question. **B** is correct. The answer is a fact directly stated in the text. You read *creamy yellow timber (see line 16)*. **A**, **C** and **D** are incorrect as they name colours that are different from creamy yellow.

2 This is a **language** question. **D** is correct. The word *prized (see line 17)* means 'highly valued'. The particular qualities of the Huon pine mean it is in high demand as a timber for boat building. **A** is incorrect because the timber is not just looked at, it is also valued for the qualities it has as a timber for boat building. **B** is incorrect as there is no evidence in the text of the timber being decorated. **C** is incorrect because the timber is not wondered about but valued highly.

3 This is a **language** question. **A** is correct. The grammar of the sentence shows that *piners (see line 12)* do the action of logging and selling trees. Words with the affix *er* are often nouns describing a person's work. **B** is incorrect because *piners* are the actors in the sentence and the trees the material they act upon, not the other way around. **C** and **D** rely on a sense of the word *pine*, meaning 'miss someone or something very badly', and this is not how it is used here.

4 This is a **synthesis** question. **C** is correct. First Sarah Island was established as a penal colony. Some time later convicts built boats there for the Government. (**A**). Later in the century logging was done commercially (**D**) and in recent times Forestry Tasmania has taken over management of 15 per cent of Huon pine trees (**B**).

5 This is an **inferring** question. **B** and **D** are correct. You infer that having natural oils and being resistant to insects and decay mean Huon pine will last for a long time and not rot quickly in water. This makes it a good boat-building timber. **A** and **C** are incorrect. **A** is true and **C** is untrue but neither are reasons that explain why Huon pine is a good timber for boat building.

6 This is a **judgement** question. You may judge that Huon pine is scarce because:
   - the Huon pine grows so slowly that when a tree is cut down it takes up to 1000 years to grow another in its place
   - it reproduces slowly
   - it only grows in parts of Tasmania
   - it is in high demand.

To Make Crumbobblious Cutlets (page 91)

1 A **2** B **3** A, B and C **4** A and C
5 A and B **6** See below

Explanations

1 This is a **language** question. **A** is correct. The word which is not a synonym for *procure* (see line 2) is 'eat'. The text says *Procure some strips of beef …* The word *procure* in the context of the recipe means 'get'. 'Obtain', 'get' and 'find' are synonyms for *procure*, which makes **B**, **C** and **D** incorrect.

2 This is a **language** question. **B** is correct. The recipe directs the reader to stir *rapidly and capriciously* (see line 8). This suggests that *capriciously* means something different from *rapidly*. The only word in the list that is different in meaning from *rapidly* is 'unpredictably'. This suits the context as 'unpredictably' suggests something being done in a random or unusual way. **A**, **C** and **D** are similar in meaning to *rapidly*, which makes them incorrect. The writer makes very careful word choices and is unlikely to repeat a meaning.

3 This is a **synthesis** question. **A**, **B** and **C** are correct. Lear repeatedly exaggerates (e.g. asking for 4 gallons of sauce), pretends to take recipes seriously, and includes nonsensical ideas in his recipe (e.g. leaving the mixture on a roof that is free from birds). **D** is incorrect because, while there are humorous ideas in the recipe, Lear does not literally tell jokes.

4 This is a **judgement** question. **A** and **C** are correct. Visualise the tiny size of a salt spoon, used to put a pinch of salt into your cooking. Visualise the much larger size of a soup ladle, used to scoop soup into bowls for serving. Now visualise trying to stir soup *rapidly* (see line 8) with either spoon. You can judge that stirring the mixture *rapidly* with either spoon would create chaos in the kitchen (**A**). The contrast in their size creates further humour as the reader imagines the impossibility of doing this task (**C**). **B** and **D** are true but they are not facts that create humour.

5 This is a **judgement** question. **A** and **B** are correct. Visualise the different sizes of cloth and trying to serve food in either one of them. The idea of a large or small cloth trying to hold the mixture which now has 4 gallons of sauce is comical because it would not fit into the cloths (**A**) and would pour out of them (**B**). **C** is incorrect because, while it is true the cloths would need laundering, this is not part of the humour of the text. **D** is incorrect because politeness or lack of it is not part of the humour of the text.

6 This is a **synthesis** question. You need to think about the way the recipe is written and imitate this in your own recipe. You should suggest actions that could either not be followed or if followed would lead to some kind of unusual result.

Seven Little Australians (page 92)

1 C **2** A **3** C **4** C **5** A **6** See below

Explanations

1 This is a **language** question. **C** is correct. A *colony of dusty boots* (see line 2) is a group of dusty boots gathered together in one place because they need cleaning. **A** is incorrect because it is a colony of dusty boots, not of objects, and they are in a basket. **B** is incorrect because while the word *colony* means a 'settlement' in some contexts, it has a different meaning in this context. **D** is incorrect because the dusty boots are not scattered but are placed together *in one corner of the room* (see lines 2–3).

2 This is an **inferring** question. **A** is correct. You can infer that Bunty wanted to please his father because the text says he imagines *his father's delighted eyes* (see line 7) seeing the boots cleaned and in a neat row. **B** and **D** are incorrect as there is no evidence in the text that cleaning boots is a job Bunty likes or is good at doing. **C** is incorrect because although Bunty plans to put the boots in rows there is no evidence that he cleaned the boots because he liked putting things in rows.

3 This is a **synthesis** question. **C** is correct. The varnish spilled after Bunty took the varnish from the shelf (**B**), put it on the arm of the chair (**A**) and sat on the floor (**D**). This makes **B**, **A** and **D** incorrect.

4 This is an **inferring** question. **C** is correct. You can infer that Bunty felt he was being a good son to be cleaning his father's boots without being asked to do so. When he heard his father's footsteps, this caused *a look of conscious virtue* [to arrive] *on his small shiny face* (see lines 15–16). **A** is true but it is only part of what Bunty felt. He was feeling pleased about how good he was being, which is what feeling virtuous means. **B** is incorrect because he did not feel horrified until later. **D** is incorrect because there is no evidence that at this stage Bunty was worried.

5 This is a **judgement** question. **A** is correct. You can judge that Bunty didn't intend to spill the varnish but placed it carelessly on the arm of the chair where it could easily spill. **B** is incorrect because Bunty doesn't act as though he is important. **C** is incorrect because his behaviour is careless rather than deliberately naughty. **D** is incorrect because there is no evidence in the text that Bunty is dishonest.

6 This is a **synthesis** question. It seems very likely that Bunty's father will be extremely angry. Bunty has ruined his father's uniform and shirt by spilling varnish over them. You might judge that his father will punish him for daring to touch his things without permission and for acting carelessly. As the story was published in 1894 you might think the punishment could be a smacking or the strap since this type of punishment was quite common at that time.

The Triantiwontigongolope (page 93)

1 C **2** C **3** A **4** D **5** See below

Explanations

1 This is a **fact-finding** question. **B** is correct. You read *has a funny face* (see lines 15–16) and *if you … tread upon its toes* (see line 29) and *it has a snubbish nose* (see lines 30–31) which means that the Triantiwontigongolope's face, toes and nose are named. **A**, **C** and **D** are incorrect as none of these body parts are named in the poem.

2 This is a **language** question. **C** is correct. You can work out the meaning from its context. The word *sneer* (see line 32) names an action the Triantiwontigongolope dislikes because it scuttles away when it is sneered at. Smiling, winking and grinning are all actions that show approval. This means to *sneer* at someone means to look scornfully at them. **A**, **B** and **D** are incorrect as these meanings show approval and would not cause the Triantiwontigongolope to *scuttle off in shame* (see lines 32–33).

3 This is a **language** question. **A** is correct. The words are linked in the line through the repetition of the consonants *t* and *tr* creating a comical picture of the Triantiwontigongolope. This poetic device is alliteration. **B**, **C** and **D**—rhyme, rhythm and simile—are not poetic devices that repeat sounds in this way and are not used to link the words in the line. This makes them incorrect.

4 This is a **synthesis** question. **D** is correct. The poem as a whole is the poet's *little joke* (see line 50) as he confesses in the last line. From the beginning, he pretends there is such a thing as a Triantiwontigongolope and spends time describing its habits. In the end he reveals he has been playing a trick on the reader because even he, the poet, has never seen one: *and I truthfully confess / That I haven't seen it either* (see lines 42–44). **A** is incorrect as teaching the reader to pronounce the name of the Triantiwontigongolope is part of the fun of the poem but not its main purpose. **B** is incorrect as there is no evidence of science in the poem. **C** is incorrect as the poet says you get *quite a scare* (see line 20) when you first see a Triantiwontigongolope, but warning you of this danger isn't the purpose of the poem.

5 This is an **inferring** question. You read *For there isn't such an insect, though there really might have been / If the trees and grass were purple, and the sky was bottle green* (see lines 46–49). You can infer from this that, like the Triantiwontigongolope, such a world doesn't literally exist so you won't find it anywhere as a real place. The poet is suggesting that a world of this kind might come to life in your imagination, just as the Triantiwontigongolope has done. You might also say you've seen such a world in illustrations which come from the imagination of an artist.

TEXT OVERVIEW GRID

Page	Title	Type of text	Additional teaching points	Writing activity
		Fact-finding questions		
24	Cassowaries	Informative—report	Endangered animals; the language of factual reporting	Research and then write a report about an endangered Australian animal.
28	How to throw a frisbee	Informative—procedure	Instructions; verb groups	Write a set of instructions for a game.
29	Thinking	Imaginative—poem	Rhyme, rhythm and alliteration	Write a poem beginning with the words 'I think ...'
30	Didgeridoos	Informative—report	Indigenous culture; the language of reporting	Research and then write a report about the role of music, art or dance in Indigenous culture.
31	Possums break into bakery	Informative—newspaper article	Newspaper reporting; humour; paragraphing	Write an account of a funny event for your local newspaper.
		Synthesis questions		
32	Save Our Planet Workshops	Persuasive—advertisement	The language of persuasion; sustainable patterns of living	Design an advertisement for a brochure about reducing household rubbish.
36	Our excursion to Chinatown	Informative—recount	Intercultural understanding; sequencing	Write a recount of an event in your life or a trip you have taken.
37	The First Hurdle	Imaginative—narrative	Tension in narrative; paragraphing	Write the beginning of a story. Create a complication. Give your story to someone else to complete. Talk together about your story.
38	Elizabeth Hayward: a survivor	Informative—biography	Stories from the first fleet: convicts who made a contribution to society; life stories	Research and write a biography of a convict sent to Australia who became well known, such as Mary Bryant or Mary Reibey.
39	Sculpture by the Sea	Informative—newspaper article	Descriptive language; reviewing	Write a review of an exhibition or concert you have attended.
		Inferring questions		
40	Is there a Loch Ness Monster?	Persuasive—discussion	Point of view; logical argument	Write three arguments for and three against the view that children under twelve need a regular bedtime.
44	My trip to South America	Informative—email	South American countries; digital communication	Write an email to a family member about a place you have visited that you think would interest them.
45	Life cycle of the frog	Informative—report	Living things and their environments; interpreting and creating diagrams	Research the life cycle of an insect and present the information in a diagram.

Page	Title	Type of text	Additional teaching points	Writing activity
Inferring questions *(continued)*				
46	The Second Hurdle	Imaginative—narrative	Fantasy literature; mood and atmosphere	Write a story with a scary atmosphere.
47	Should you feed wild birds? (1)	Persuasive—discussion	Point of view; modality; responsible behaviour	Write a speech for a debate that argues why you should not feed wild animals.
48	My childhood memories	Imaginative—recollection	How and why daily lives change over time; personal writing	Write a list of things you remember from before you turned seven. Ask an older family member to do the same. Compare memories.
49	Should children have to earn their pocket money?	Persuasive—argument	Discussion; dialogue; ethical issues	Write a conversation between parents discussing the topic: Should children have to earn their pocket money?
50	Jim Jones at Botany Bay	Imaginative—poetry	Ballads; stories from the first fleet	Write an extra verse for the end of the ballad. Tell of Jim's arrival in Botany Bay.
51	Alice in Wonderland	Imaginative—narrative	*Alice in Wonderland* by Lewis Carroll, 1865; classic British fantasy; imaginative worlds; episodic structures	Create a different adventure for Alice when she goes down the rabbit-hole.
Language questions				
52	When Jimbo Lost His Spots	Imaginative—narrative	Fables; Dreaming stories; Pourquoi stories	Write a story about how the cockatoo got its screech or a story to explain a feature of an animal of your choice.
56	Kwanza, the white lion	Informative—diary entry	Dependence on each other of living things; diary writing	Write a diary entry about looking after an animal in your care.
57	Corroboree, Sydney	Persuasive—radio promotion	Features of spoken texts; advertising techniques	Prepare a spoken advertisement to present at a school assembly.
58	Ming the Mollusc	Imaginative—poem	Scientific methods; personification; word play in poetry	Imagine you are someone or something else for a day and write a poem about it.
59	Night Noodle Markets	Persuasive—website advertisement	Navigation of online texts; onomatopoeia	Design a webpage to advertise a festival or celebration.
60	George Raper: a short life	Informative—biography	Stories from the first fleet: flora and fauna of Australia	Research an example of Australian flora or fauna. Draw it and label its parts.
61	The Third Hurdle	Imaginative—narrative	Character development; unusual human qualities; setting	Write a story with a main character who has the ability to do something that other humans can't do.
62	Words under the microscope	Informative—report	Word histories; languages that have influenced English	Research and make a list of twenty words that have come into English from other languages, such as Aboriginal, Latin, Greek, Italian or French.
63	The seahorse	Imaginative—narrative; Informative—report	Sea creatures; animal behaviour; first-person narration	Research a sea creature. Imagine you are that sea creature and explain what your life is like.

Page	Title	Type of text	Additional teaching points	Writing activity
		Judgement questions		
64	Peter Pan	Imaginative—narrative	*Peter Pan* by JM Barrie, 1911; classic British fantasy; stories in different media	Choose a book that has been made into a film. Write a review of the film. Make sure you discuss the characters.
68	The day I disappeared	Imaginative—narrative	First-person narrative; sequencing events	Write a song about feeling lonely.
69	The advantages and disadvantages of the internet	Persuasive—discussion	The language of opinion; construction of charts	Interview some adults about the disadvantages of technology. Report their responses in chart form.
70	Camouflage in the animal kingdom	Informative—report	Survival of living things; varieties of vegetation	Research and write a report about an animal which uses camouflage effectively.
71	The clockwork insect	Informative—newspaper article	Insects and their movements; technical language	Record your observations of an insect's or spider's movements and behaviour.
72	Anthony Browne's *King Kong*	Persuasive—discussion	Emotive language; comparison of texts	Write a conversation between two people discussing different opinions of a picture book.
73	The Rainbow Dragon's Lair	Imaginative—narrative	Mood and atmosphere; figurative language	Write a story that has a mythical beast that can be tricked.
74	That it is a waste of money to develop robots	Persuasive—discussion	Arguments for and against; fact and opinion	Invent an imaginary robot. Make a list of arguments defending the view that production of your robot deserves to be funded.
75	Could it have happened?	Informative—newspaper article	Journeys of world navigators before the 18th century; credible argument; modality	Write two texts that present different points of view on an event in history.
		Mixed questions		
76	How is glass made?	Informative—explanation	Properties of processed materials; explanations	Research how plastic is made and write an explanation about it for a younger group of students.
77	Ratty times	Imaginative—drama	Conditions on the first fleet; dialogue; punctuation	Write a playscript that includes a conversation between two or three convicts who are on their way to Australia.
78	Woollarawarre Bennelong (c.1764–1813)	Informative—biography	Contact between Aboriginal people and early settlers; Aboriginal peoples	Write a biography of an Aboriginal or Torres Strait Islander person.
79	The Wonderful Wizard of Oz	Imaginative—narrative	*The Wonderful Wizard of Oz* by L Frank Baum, 1900; classic American fantasy/ adventure	Write a draft of the opening of a fantasy or adventure. Record yourself reading it aloud. Listen to your reading and then improve your draft.
80	Talking about books	Persuasive—discussion	Formal and informal language; evaluative language	Write a conversation between two children about a popular author and/ or illustrator.
81	The age of discovery	Informative—report	Journeys of exploration in the age of discovery; factual information; context	Imagine you are a navigator or explorer living in the 16th or 17th century. Write a report of your most famous journey.

Page	Title	Type of text	Additional teaching points	Writing activity
		Mixed Questions *(continued)*		
82	Should you feed wild birds? (2)	Persuasive—discussion	Living things and their environments; responsible and ethical behaviour.	List two or three arguments for and against removing animals from the wild.
83	My trip to China	Informative—email	Cultural understanding; sustainability	Research a Chinese artefact, such as a building or sculpture of cultural significance, and write a description of it.
84	The Ugly Animal Protection Society	Persuasive—discussion	Prejudice; stereotypes; cohesion in texts	Write a speech about the saying 'You can't judge a book by its cover'.
85	Barangaroo	Informative—biography	Life of Aboriginal people after colonisation; summaries	Write an account of the life of a female you admire.
86	Marianne Musgrave's *The Worry Tree*	Persuasive—review	Plot tension; ethical and responsible behaviour	Describe a problem you or someone else has had and explain how it was solved.
87	New Year's resolutions	Imaginative—diary entry	Expression of personal thoughts; the first person	List five New Year's resolutions you'd like to make for yourself or others.
88	Come to the Alice	Persuasive—advertisement	Emotive language; the second person; audiences	Design an advertisement to persuade families to visit an Australian city.
89	Idioms	Informative—report	Language devices; literal and inferred meanings	Interview family members about the idioms they use when speaking in their home language. Write a report of your findings.
90	Huon pine	Informative—report	Properties of natural materials; the language of reporting	Research and write a report about bamboo: Where does it come from? How does it grow? What is it used for?
91	To Make Crumbobblious Cutlets	Imaginative—recipe	*To Make Crumbobblious Cutlets* by Edward Lear, 1870; types of humour (e.g. exaggeration, puns, send-up, wordplay)	Write a send-up of instructions for cooking a cake.
92	Seven Little Australians	Imaginative—novel	*Seven Little Australians* by Ethel Turner, 1894; classic Australian family story; setting and context	Write a story, poem or play set around 100 years ago.
93	The Triantiwonti-gongolope	Imaginative—poetry	*The Triantiwontigongolope* by CJ Dennis, 1821; rhyme, rhythm and humour in poetry	Invent an imaginary insect and write a poem about it. You may like to imitate the rhyme and rhythm of a published poem.